EDGAR CAYCE ON
MYSTERIES OF THE MIND

The unlimited scope of human consciousness

EDGAR CAYCE ON MYSTERIES OF THE MIND

HENRY REED

Edited by CHARLES THOMAS CAYCE

Aquarian/Thorsons

An Imprint of HarperCollins*Publishers*

The Aquarian Press
An Imprint of HarperCollins*Publishers*
77–85 Fulham Palace Road,
Hammersmith, London W6 8JB

First UK edition 1990
This edition published by arrangement with
Warner Books, Inc., New York
3 5 7 9 10 8 6 4 2

© The Association for Research and
Enlightenment, Inc. 1989

A catalogue record for this book
is available from the British Library

ISBN 0 85030 861 5

Printed in Great Britain by
HarperCollinsManufacturing Glasgow

All rights reserved. No part of this publication may be
reproduced, stored in a retrieval system, or transmitted,
in any form or by any means, electronic, mechanical,
photocopying, recording or otherwise, without the prior
permission of the publishers.

Table of Contents

INTRODUCTION

Looking Into the Mirror of the Mind

It doesn't seem possible, but it happened. It made electron microscopes, radio telescopes, radioactive carbon dating, and CAT scans, not to mention television and the telephone, seem trivial and unimportant or unnecessary. What kind of sophisticated electronic equipment do you think you would need to read a book that is sitting unopened in a distant library, to tell your friend what is happening to the atoms of his or her body, or to remember what happened thousands and thousands of years ago? Simply by lying down, relaxing, closing his eyes, and transporting himself from the limits of consciousness, Edgar Cayce was able to enter a superconscious trance state that made all these marvels of modern technology seem clumsy.

As a child, Cayce could sleep on a textbook and awaken with a photographic memory of its contents, without once having opened the book. As he grew and developed his gifts, he could diagnose the illnesses of people he had never met and otherwise knew nothing about. Moreover, his diagnoses included minute facts about the workings of the body that would take scientific medicine years to verify. With his farseeing eye he could locate an obscure medicine on the dusty stockroom shelf of a faraway pharmacy so that it could be located and used to help someone. His memory traveled far back into time and revealed the personal experiences of those who walked the planet before our recorded history. He went even further back and described the formation of the earth.

From this state of infinite knowing, Cayce claimed that he was doing nothing special, but something we could do ourselves. Although astonishing beyond belief, he indicated that all knowledge, that's right, *all*, is within. You and I already have within ourselves every bit of knowledge that has ever been known, as well as the seeds of all that will ever be known. It is all within, inside our own mind.

The mind is as infinite as the universe. No matter how far into outer space you can send your imagination, you still have not reached the boundaries of the mind. Nothing except creation itself is as unbounded and infinite as the mind—your mind, my mind. Explore it and you will see.

Before we can even catch our breath at the thought of an infinite mind, Cayce delivers another surprise. The mind not only is receptive, but active. It is creative. It creates the world that we live in. It gives form to the plants and animals, the rocks and the ocean, our bodies and our lives. Our minds create our experiences, our reality. The mind has an infinite capacity to know the world, because the mind created it.

How can this invisible, untouchable, seemingly unknowable thing we call the mind have such powers? How can it be? And if it is so, what does that mean for the way we live our lives? What are we to do with this knowledge? If it is so, it is so profound and fundamental a reality that it must completely upset all the ways we normally think of living or approach having a life. If there is something inside of you and I that is as immense as the universe and more powerful than any atomic bomb yet invented, how in the world could it possibly fit within our bodies? How does it get scrunched up inside our small skulls and how does it get out to do its magic?

Claiming these mysterious powers of the mind must be some form of poetic statement, not a literal truth. It couldn't be literally true.

But it is. And it has practical implications. As practical as staying healthy or finding a job. As practical as quitting smoking or getting along with people. It also has its spiritual side. Nothing is as essentially spiritual as learning to love. Nothing is as important to the development of our spiritual awareness as investing the gift of life with our own constructive efforts to nurture it. Thus the range of the implications runs the spectrum from the mundane to the spiritual. All this is contained within the mysteries of the mind.

Cayce's ideas about the mind, as farfetched as they may seem at first glance, have been receiving increased attention in recent years, as he predicted. As the twentieth century comes to a close, the many pressures and threats to our survival on this planet have been counterbalanced by much research and new thinking about the nature of mind and its role in our future. Research in many laboratories has verified many of Cayce's ideas. Theorists have developed perspectives on the mind that are similar to Cayce's view.

This book is the result of this scientific progress, for it is now possible to share the secrets revealed by Cayce in a way that is supported by scientific research.

Not only does scientific research now support the creative powers of the mind, but also hundreds of books, videotapes, audiocassettes, workshops, and seminars teach these principles. Many of the ideas first proposed by Cayce are now almost mainstream. Who hasn't heard of the power of positive thinking? Creative visualization and subliminal suggestion are now common items on the marketplace. The healing power of optimism and humor is routinely discussed on TV talk shows. Is there anything newsworthy left among the legacy of the Cayce readings?

Cayce continues to provide us with a new look at the mysteries of the mind. His body of work remains the only single source that provides a complete model, ranging from the spiritual to the atom, based on a few encompassing principles. Cayce was a pioneer in explaining matters of the spirit in psychological terms. The Eastern traditions have had their Yoga psychology for thousands of years, but Westerners have lacked an approach to the mystical side of life that was simultaneously compatible with their scientific worldview. Cayce's readings provided that approach. His was an integrated view, from the consciousness of the individual cell in the body to the holographic reality of the human soul. His was a practical view, providing the steps to take, suggesting techniques to use. His was what scientists call an "empirical" approach, meaning an emphasis on the facts of experience. He didn't ask that anyone believe what he said; in fact, he discouraged it. He didn't want your belief; he wanted you to experiment, to test his ideas in practice. Only what you have made your own through personal application is of any value. As I prepared for this book, looking through my files of research reports for experimental evidence corresponding to his ideas, browsing through libraries and bookstores stocked with books on the powers of the mind, and reflected on my own experiences developing my personal skills in this area, I was surprised to discover just how many important ideas and perspectives the Cayce material adds to the current culture of ideas on the powers of the mind.

A popular item on the market today, for example, is "subliminal suggestion" self-help tapes. Cayce was an advocate of the use of suggestion. He would applaud the technology of the cassette player that allows us to listen to suggestions that we ourselves design. He also recognized the power of subliminal suggestion. He saw it as a more active influence in our lives than we might suspect. As you learn more about our vulnerability to psychic influence, you will appreciate his surprising warning about the use of such methods as subliminal suggestion.

It is popular today to speak of "creating your own reality." That philosophy, as old as the first mystical experience, has taken on heroic proportions with the advent of our modern psychological technology of human growth. Yet it brings to the contemporary person its own set of new problems. Does it have any limits? Can I have anything I want? Does that mean I am to blame for my troubles? Those of us susceptible to the pitfalls of the "me generation" find creating our own reality leading us into a hall of mirrors. Everywhere we look, all we see is ourselves. Cayce's view adds a critical ingredient to the creation of reality formula that leads us out of the moral predicament of egocentricity without diminishing the incredible magic of our creative power. His perspective on this philosophy helps us get beyond ourselves, but without our leaving ourselves behind.

Self-help psychology has been with us for several decades. With the advent of the New Age perspective, however, the promises that are offered have become more optimistic and all-encompassing than ever before. For someone who doubts, or doesn't feel quite up to such heroic changes and self-improvement, these upbeat philosophies can be somewhat threatening. It's easy to feel that you'll never be enthusiastic enough, good enough, skillful enough to pull off such miracles of self-transformation yourself. Edgar Cayce's perspective, however, is intended to help even the most determined of self-doubters.

Although his psychic perspective reaches far into the heavens and deep within the soul, it is also grounded in the

day-to-day rhythm of our emotional lives and the limitations
we find there. While he suggests we can fly to the moon, he
also points out the value of taking a simple step forward in
our earthly life. Although he wants us to become aware of
all the mysteries that the mind has to offer, he also assures
us that there is nothing more important than loving those
around us. While he explains how the powers of the mind
can be used to extricate us from even the most impossible of
situations, he realizes that all we might be able to manage
for the moment is to slightly loosen the grip of such
circumstances. Peace of mind, no matter how momentary, is
of great value.

Above all, Cayce encourages us to make a start. Over and
over he repeats this promise: If you will just do one thing
that you know to do, if you will take but one step forward,
something will happen to make the second step easier.
There is a power within you greater than you realize. It
awaits you, now.

1

It's All in the Mind

For the time has arisen in the earth when men—
everywhere—seek to know more of the mysteries
of the mind, the soul, the soul's mind.
Edgar Cayce 254-52

What does the expression "It's all in your mind" mean to you? Ask many people and the answer is something like "Imaginary... not real." Do they think the mind is imaginary or not real? Not exactly. Many people *do* think that reality is one thing and the mind is another. As, for example, when the mind sometimes misses the mark and imagines something as real when it is not. Isn't that a fair description of the usual meaning of "It's all in the mind"?

Yet there is a totally different meaning to this maxim. This other meaning begins to appear when the mind is explored for its mysteries. The phrase becomes a teaser, almost a riddle. It becomes an invitation for you to discover a way to take command of your life and "have it your way." Let's see how that happens.

Common Mysteries

The mind usually seems more invisible than mysterious. Most of the time we hardly notice it's there. But there are those moments when we become aware of the mind. Sometimes strange events bring it to our attention. I'm sure you've experienced some of these very common little mysteries.

For example, you have been driving along the highway, returning home. As you approach your neighborhood, you realize that for the past several minutes your mind has been elsewhere. Daydreaming, thinking about things, your mind has been on anything but paying attention to the road. You wonder how you managed to watch out for cars, follow traffic signals, and make the right turns when you weren't even "there." There are a number of things we do without paying attention.

Suppose you are working on a problem and it has you stumped. Maybe it's about how to rearrange the furniture in your house, or it could be about designing a new procedure at the office. Nothing that you can come up with seems quite right. One day. in the middle of a conversation, or while out shopping ьr taking a walk, an idea suddenly comes to you like a bolt out of the blue. A perfect solution to the problem is simply handed to you, without apparent effort. You weren't even thinking about it. Perhaps there is another part of the mind outside of your awareness.

For no apparent reason, for example, you find yourself thinking of an old friend. Later that day, you receive a letter from that person, or the person calls you up on the phone. It was almost as if you were in mental contact or somehow knew the person was going to call. Perhaps the mind can reach out and touch someone without telephoning long-distance.

Another time you are sitting with someone having a cup of coffee when a remark is made that triggers a strange sensation. You have this odd feeling that you are reliving some experience from the past. You seem to know what the person will say next. It's as if you are repeating a scene you have lived before, even though you cannot remember when it was. Does the mind also reach beyond time?

You had a dream. Dreams seem real at the time. As a child, you may have wondered how it was possible to be fooled that way. As an adult you may be used to ignoring dreams, and would have forgotten about this dream. Maybe it was of a seemingly ordinary, everyday event, or it may have been an upsetting dream about something bad happening. A few days later, perhaps a few weeks later, the dream comes true. Many of the details of the event are just like what was in the dream. Was the dream real? Can the mind determine what is real?

We've all been in lousy moods. You know what it's like to be kind of depressed, a bit lonely. You've felt sorry for yourself sometimes because of your problems. At times they seem overpowering and unbeatable. You've probably also had those occasions where somehow you find yourself feeling better about things even though your problems haven't changed. Maybe you encountered someone who was in a really bad way and you reached out to the person and provided some cheer. Maybe you went to a comedy movie and laughed until your sides hurt. Maybe it was something else. But later you realize that your own mood has lifted. Your problems are still there, but somehow you feel better anyway. You look at the same facts with a different slant and you see things differently. It's almost as if you've changed your mind about what's real.

All these experiences are actually quite common. Some may seem easy to explain; others are perhaps more puzzling. Yet they all suggest that the mind is not as simple as it seems.

We take the mind for granted. We assume it is like a mirror that reflects the reality in front of us. It seems it is fed information by our five senses. We use the mind to think. Our thoughts feel as if we are talking to ourself silently. But where is the mind? Can you point to it or touch it? Is it in the brain? If so, then how do minds that are contained within skulls "meet" during those moments of intimate conversation? Just what kind of "stuff" is the mind? These kinds of questions show that the mind is actually the most puzzling mystery human beings have ever encountered.

Forgetting: Accidental or On Purpose?

Memory is one of those things that sometimes make us realize what a puzzle the mind can be.

How often do we make a promise to ourselves but fail to keep it? How many good intentions are "forgotten"? There are many things that we know would be good for us, that would increase the quality of our lives—relaxing, spending time with the family, perhaps taking up a new sport, developing different dietary habits. Yet we have trouble remembering to do them. There just isn't enough time in the day, and we "forget" those good things.

How often we find ourselves in a spot when we want to remember something but can't. Ever misplaced something and tried to remember where you put it? How is it that we have memories that we cannot recall when we want to, like a person's name, but which sometimes pop up all on their own? Apparently, the memories are there. Sometimes they just appear out of nowhere, clear as a bell. Often, however, they are unavailable to us. Yet they can still have their effect.

A colleague of mine once remarked that there is a strange

irony to memory. On the one hand, our childhood experiences exert a powerful effect upon our adult personality and how we view the world. Yet the memories of these experiences are almost impossible to bring to the surface. How can something that we cannot remember have such a strong influence?

Forgetting can be such a problem that it is tempting to wish for a perfect memory. Yet our memory is already more perfect than you might suspect. And forgetting can play a useful role for us. What would memory be without forgetting? Who would want a pencil without an eraser? There are some things we want to forget. If you could not forget for the moment all the things that you *should* be doing right now, how could you concentrate on reading this book? Forgetting can be as important as remembering. It would be ideal to have both of these under our control, rather than our being at their mercy.

Learning how to forget can perhaps be as useful as learning to remember. Take a clue from a familiar, eccentric hero: the world's original detective, Sherlock Holmes.

He had just learned what he considered to be a piece of trivia. Although he was a gold mine of information, there were many surprising gaps in his knowledge. Dr. Watson had just informed him, in *A Study in Scarlet*, that the earth and several other planets with it revolved around the sun. Holmes replied that having heard this little tidbit, he would now promptly forget it—on purpose. He explained to the startled Watson that useless facts take up as much room in one's memory as does important information. By deliberately forgetting the trivial, he could more easily concentrate on the important.

Sherlock Holmes knew that the controlled use of his mind was the key to his success. He had learned that just as the mind can be trained to remember desired facts, so also can it be trained to forget.

Do you know Holmes's secret? Do you know how to forget on purpose? Can you do it at will? Can you control the process of forgetting and use it to your advantage? Suppose I tell you that the capital of Bolivia is La Paz. Now, can you forget it, the way Sherlock could? How would you go about it? Try it. Have you forgotten it yet? What is the capital of Bolivia? It's much like the old challenge to not think of the eye of an elephant. Once it's mentioned, you immediately see it in your mind. How can you get something out of your mind when you want to?

I studied this problem, as a graduate student of psychology at UCLA, and it proved to be my introduction to the mysteries of the mind. My mentor, Bernard Weiner, had discovered that people can forget on purpose. He was trying to figure out how they did it. He would give a person a word to read on a screen and then tell them to forget it. Here's a word for you to read:

Table

Now I want you to forget it. While you try, I'll continue describing our research as you read on.

If we gave people a word to forget and asked them to simply sit there and try to forget it, they just couldn't do it. However, after they saw the word to forget, if we then gave them additional material to read, they were more successful at forgetting the original word.

What about the word you just read a moment ago—do you still remember it, or have you been able to forget it while reading this paragraph? In our experiments, the chances were about fifty-fifty that a person would have successfully forgotten the word.

How do people forget on purpose? How did you go about trying to forget? It seems that the most natural approach is to try to think of something else. Did you, for example, try to concentrate on the reading, hoping that meanwhile the word would disappear from your mind? Trying to think of one thing in order to press something else out of the mind seems to be the way we try to forget.

Without doubting Sherlock's genius, we should rephrase his method by stating that in order to forget the trivial, *concentrate on the essential!* Focus on what you want your mind to retain, and what you want to forget will pass away. We will encounter many variations on this principle throughout this book.

Sherlock Holmes wanted to forget in order to keep his mind uncluttered. We often have other reasons to forget something. We might wish to forget a bad habit. Wouldn't it be nice to learn how to "forget to smoke" rather than having to struggle with willpower to fight the urge to smoke? What bad habit do you wish you could simply forget?

Sometimes we are bothered by something we can't do anything about. It would be pleasant to simply be able to forget about it.

In the book *The Little Prince*, the young hero visits several different planets. On one he encounters a drunkard sitting at a table with his bottle and cup. He asks the fellow why he drinks so much. The red-nosed fellow says he drinks to forget! How many times have we all used alcohol, drugs, or other forms of escape, such as shopping or watching TV, to forget our worries? By focusing on something else, we hope that our troubles will disappear from our mind. We all use a rough approximation of Sherlock's secret. We can learn to perfect this method to our better advantage.

Come On, Get Happy!

Peace of mind is perhaps one of life's most elusive treasures. Those who have found it value it highly. Most of

us wish for it, but the pressures and uncertainties of modern
life make it difficult. It is hard to ignore our problems.
Many things that we would like to forget haunt us. Yet some
people find that they can forget their worries by concentrating on something else, something positive or cheerful.
That's how they get happy and stay that way.

You've heard about the value of keeping a positive
attitude—it's called "looking on the bright side." You've
probably experimented with this strategy yourself at various
times. It may seem like a pleasant suggestion—it can't
hurt—but of little use in actually dealing with problem
situations. Attitude, however—that certain slant of mind
that determines how we view things—has proven to have
tremendous power.

Consider the case of people who have been confronted
with a major trauma or disaster in life. I'm talking about
being held as a prisoner of war, being taken hostage by
terrorists or kidnappers, getting lost on a frozen mountaintop or down inside a mine shaft, having one's home destroyed
by a tornado, or having one's life ransacked by a terrible
disease. The victims of such catastrophes are often never the
same afterward. It's as if they also lose something on the
inside as a result of the ordeal. Social scientists have studied
people who have gone through such traumas and catastrophes. While some people are destroyed by the experience,
others survive and rebuild their lives. What seems to make
the difference between succumbing or surviving is the attitude that was adopted during the ordeal.

Those who did not survive fell victim to an attitude of
helplessness. It's an understandable reaction. Control over
their lives had been stolen from them. There was little that
they could do about the situation. The dark side of their
predicament became imprinted on their mind.

Those who survived, however, managed to adopt a different attitude. They fought the temptation to give up and

looked for some way to regain some small bit of personal control. Even being able to make decisions about a trivial aspect of their situation made a difference in their mental outlook. They searched hard for some way to look upon the bright side.

The psychology of survivors proves that a mental attitude can have a definite effect on how we deal with problems. It can make the difference between being victimized by problems or learning from them how to survive, and much more.

Surviving Daily Life

Ordinary life has its own ups and downs. On good days, when things are going our way, we're on top of the world. On bad days, it's not so good. Nothing is as we would have it, and life becomes a real struggle. We certainly don't feel on top of things; they feel on top of us.

On good days, we might say, "Life couldn't be better if I designed it myself!" On bad days, life can seem like a cruel joke. The joke is on us, and we become the tragic victim of circumstances.

The difference between the good times and the bad seems to be whether or not things are going our way.

On good days, you're on a roll and everything you do turns out well. You have hunches that pan out. Coincidences occur that make the day seem designed for you. Your every wish comes true. On days like that, you get the sensation that you can actually create the kind of life you would like to live. Life is like a fun movie and you get to write the script.

On the bad days, you feel helpless and out of control. You have no choices, you are under pressure, between a rock and a hard place, more is being expected of you than you can deliver, forced to do something you would rather not, and about to lose something you value—these are the sorts of things that make life seem like a mindless machine wearing you down.

It's almost as if there are two realities, two types of life. In one reality, we are victims, we have to take what comes and cope the best we can. Sometimes the odds are against us. The best we can do is to minimize our losses. Life is bigger than us and has us caught in its grip. Life acts and we react.

In the other reality, it seems the reverse. We act and life reacts. We get to design the day our way. We become the scriptwriter, director, and actor upon the stage of life.

Which is the true reality? It may be clear which one we prefer, but which reality is the way life really is? Is there an answer to that question? Is it just what you want to believe?

Believing in the Possible

Suppose I were to ask you to assume that believing is everything. Suppose that it does make a difference what you believe. What if you were to believe that your mind creates the world you live in, the kind of day you have and the life you live. If you believe you can, you can create a good day or a bad day and take charge of your life. You can design your life the way you want it, because the mind creates the kind of life you have. If that were true, wouldn't it be an important thing to know?

Just think, if it were really not true that life comes to us on its own terms and we have to take what comes, wouldn't it be important to know that? If it were true that we can design life to our own patterns, wouldn't you like to know that? Couldn't you use that fact to your advantage?

I know it may not seem true. It's too hard to believe. For now I would like simply to suggest that the idea is important. It certainly is worth considering. It has important implications for your life. You may not be able to believe in the possibility yet, but do not insist that it is impossible. What we believe has important consequences. I'm sure you've heard of self-fulfilling prophecies.

We know a lot about self-fulfilling prophecies. Repeated classroom research has proven, for example, that students from whom their teachers expect good work do good work, while students whom the teacher believe cannot do well usually don't. Have you ever experienced the power of having someone really believe in you? It can be a wonderful source of support. On the other hand, we can feel uncomfortable around someone who believes only in our weaknesses. It makes us feel insecure, and sometimes we find ourselves stumbling. The expectation is confirmed.

What are the limits of this power of belief? Science is just beginning to explore the outer limits of this mystery. The power of belief is actually quite stronger than you might realize.

In medical history, for example, there is the well-known story of a Mr. Wright who had terminal cancer. He believed that there was going to be a drug that would cure him. He heard that his hospital was testing the experimental drug, Krebiozen, and he became convinced that this was the drug that was going to save his life.

Mr. Wright repeatedly requested that his doctor use the drug on his case. Finally, the doctor relented and gave it to him. Unlike the experimental patients, who were showing little response to treatment by Krebiozen, Mr. Wright made a rapid recovery and his cancer went away. He left the hospital and returned to a normal life.

Then Mr. Wright read in the newspaper that Krebiozen was proving ineffective against cancer. Within days, Mr. Wright's cancer returned to its former condition.

Mr. Wright's doctor decided on an experiment and told

him that they had found that the problem with the Krebiozen was that it had a short shelf life. The medicine that had been used on him was old, the doctor said, but there was a fresh batch that could now be administered. This time he was given only plain water, but it provided him an even more miraculously quick and complete cure. He left the hospital once more to resume his life.

Unfortunately, Mr. Wright later read in the newspaper that scientists had proven without a doubt that the Krebiozen was worthless. His cancer returned and he died a few days later. In his case, and in many others like his, belief held the power of life and death.

From the Imagination to Reality

Belief and expectation have a powerful effect. If the power of belief, as evidenced in the case of Mr. Wright, could be bottled and sold, it would be a wonder drug. Actually, the power has already been bottled. It is in your mind. It is contained in the imagination.

Look around you. How many things can you see that first existed in someone's imagination before they existed in physical reality? Houses, cars, and clothing, to name but a few. All these human inventions were first ideas. They came from the mind.

Have you ever been to Disneyland or Disney World? Did you ever think how the world of Disney was first an idea in the imagination of Walt Disney? He began drawing cartoons and wondered how he could bring them to life. At the time, animated cartoons were just being invented. Disney worked hard to develop the technology of that art form. He finally brought Mickey Mouse to life out of his mind. When we watch Mickey Mouse in a cartoon, the character seems real. The child in you believes him to be real. And the holographic,

3-D cartoons that can now be produced make Mickey even more real. It all originated in the imagination of Walt Disney.

Imagination, together with a positive attitude and belief or expectancy, is a powerful combination. Just think of how many inventions that make our world as wonderful as it is came from this special combination we sometimes call "visionary determination"—the light bulb, the airplane, spacecraft, and surely you can think of many more.

The imagination, in fact, is the way to direct the positive energy of belief and attitude. With the imagination, we can do things that even today, before reading this book, you would have believed impossible.

Consider the case of Garrett Porter. When he was ten years old, he was told that he had an inoperable brain tumor. Radiation therapy did little good. He was going to die.

Garrett was fortunate enough to be in Topeka, Kansas, where the Menninger Clinic is located. Pat Norris, a psychologist at the clinic, was conducting research on the role of the imagination in healing. She taught Garrett how to use his imagination, in a specially concentrated form, to direct his body to destroy the cancer cells in his brain. They worked against time, day after day.

Once or twice a day, Garrett imagined the white cells in his bloodstream eating up the cancer cells. One day Garrett announced that he could no longer find his brain tumor in his imagination. A CAT scan of his brain confirmed the information provided by his imagination—the tumor was gone. He and Dr. Norris wrote their story, *I Choose Life*, so that other people can learn how there is hope.

Garrett's story is an example of the mind's directly changing the reality of the body. The mind took control and erased the tumor. Sometimes we think that a positive attitude, looking on the bright side or imagining the possible, is only a sweetener, that it adds a spoonful of sugar to help the medicine go down but otherwise has no effects. Garrett's story shows that a positive attitude can be more than simply adding a spoonful of sugar to the medicine. It was not simply making a bad situation more tolerable. Garret changed the reality. The tumor was gone. The mind has the ability to control the events in the body.

The stories of Mr. Wright and Garrett Porter may seem like something out of *The Twilight Zone*. They are just too impossible to be true. But they are true. And they are not the only stories. The secret powers of the mind have been verified in laboratories and clinics all over the world, and more is being discovered every day.

The Consciousness Revolution

Things haven't been the same since the sixties. Something happened back then that has changed the way we have viewed the world ever since. It was the beginning of the "consciousness revolution."

It was the era of the Vietnam war, whose horrors, frustrations, contradictions, and confusions gave birth to the term "burnout." As the end result of a chronic gridlock of stress, fatigue, and discouragement created in the face of conflicting ideals and contradictory expectations, burnout has become a familiar word in many areas of today's life. It has led to an intense reevaluation of many of our assumptions. As old solutions no longer work there has now developed a realization that "trying harder" needs to be replaced by "trying smarter." Different approaches are needed that require a new way of looking at things.

As part of the shake-up of the times, the sixties also witnessed the explosion of the psychedelic scene. The use of drugs was not what was so uniquely influential about psychedelics. People have always gotten drugged, and we've

always known that it isn't healthy. What was significant was
that it was psychedelic drugs that were being used. The
word means "mind-manifesting." These were drugs that
"turned on" the otherwise invisible mind so that it could be
seen. Psychedelic drugs revealed to many people in a
dramatic fashion that the mind is an important and creative
reality in itself. The fortunate ones got the message quickly
and then turned to other methods of exploring the mysteries
of the mind. Many people graduated from marijuana, not to
heroin, but to meditation.

Among them were the Beatles. As they opened a new
frontier in music and a new role for it in society, we
watched them go from turning on with drugs to visits with
the Maharishi. In their movie *Yellow Submarine* they announce the secret that becomes a time bomb for our lives:
"It's all in the mind."

Beatle fans knew what was being said. There was the
suggestion of "make-believe," as the animation effects of
their movie made so startlingly clear. Yet there was also the
understanding that a deeper secret was being revealed—the
mind is both the origin and purpose of reality. All that
we seek for can be found within ourselves. The love that we
long to receive from others originates from the love we
grow from within our own hearts. Ancient truths, actually,
but now delivered by our culture's pop heroes on the large
cinema screen and across the airwaves.

Twenty some years later, Shirley MacLaine announced
on her television miniseries *Out On a Limb*, "You create
your own reality." It is the Beatles' statement recast in a
new vocabulary. Yet of the millions of viewers who watched
this program, many seemed confounded if not outraged by
her remarks. For a week afterward, I heard men in the steam
room, who usually discuss only sports, sweating Shirley's
story out of their system. For months, Shirley became
comedy material for Johnny Carson and others. Clearly she

touched a nerve, even if some misunderstood her message.

Yet there were many who found her show to be but a rerun of experiences they had had themselves and of ideas they believed in. In the two decades between the Beatles and Shirley MacLaine, in laboratories around the world, reported in books by the thousands and workshops and classes galore, the consciousness revolution had sprouted, planted roots, and borne many fruits. The neuroscience of the brain, the psychology of meditation, these and many other disciplines of study were accumulating facts and proving theories that point to new ideas about the mind. The provocative statements made earlier by the Beatles and now by Shirley MacLaine were being supported.

Edgar Cayce: The "Sleeping Prophet"

It was during the sixties, when I was in one of those laboratories working on the mystery of memory, that I was introduced to the work of Edgar Cayce. I was interested in the problem of amnesia, wondering how a person could forget their own identify and life history. I had decided to explore an everyday amnesia, the forgetting of dreams, where one's nighttime experiences are forgotten by morning. Did sleep have something to do with the forgetting? Could hypnosis bring the memories back? These were the questions I was contemplating when a friend brought me a book about Edgar Cayce and what he had to say about dreams. What I read changed the course of my life and work.

I discovered first that Edgar Cayce learned how to enter a self-induced hypnotic sleep. He would be amnesic later for what transpired during this sleep. On the other hand, while in this altered state of consciousness, his memory was immense. It went beyond his own personal experiences, to encompass events in history and other people's experiences dating back thousands of years. He entered a state of superconsciousness, showing an understanding of things that surpassed his humble waking state. In his waking life, he was a photographer and a Sunday-school teacher. But while in this special trance, he became "the sleeping prophet."

He was best known for diagnosing illnesses. Given simply the name of someone at a distant location, he could describe the person's illness and prescribe treatments. At the time of his work, between the years 1901 and 1944, his treatments sounded strange. Today he is recognized as the father of holistic medicine, that approach to healing that treats the whole person—body, mind, and spirit.

I found particularly important Cayce's psychology. In his superconscious state he presented a different view of the mind than I had learned in school. Yet his ideas seemed very important, because they helped to make sense out of many of the common mysteries of the mind that I wanted to understand. He also said that we are all amnesic for the powers of the mind, but that we could awaken to them and use them for our benefit.

I was amazed at what Edgar Cayce had to say. I began a search in the library to find out more about what he did. Was he a freak? I discovered that history contains the stories of other people like him. Many people had discovered that behind the normal waking mind there lies another, more knowledgeable, consciousness. I found that this superconscious mind, regardless of who it is speaking through, has surprisingly similar things to say about the psychology of the mind. I learned that what made Cayce unique was that he took these lessons from the superconscious mind to heart in his own life. By applying them in his daily affairs, he developed himself to be even better able to receive inspirations from the superconscious source. His primary motivation was to be able to obtain information that people could use to better their lives.

A New Look at The Mysteries of Mind

Although it seemed that Cayce's sleeping state was a very magical state of mind, it had a simple message for you and me. It was that the mind Cayce was using in his special sleep is the same mind that exists within each of us. It's there, waiting to be called upon, already active within us. It's active every night during our dreams. It is also available to us in other ways during the day.

The mind is not a mirror of reality. It is more like a holographic studio, creating images and projecting them through consciousness to become what we take to be reality. The mind does more than watch life go by; it does more than spin mental computations. The mind is a living, active, *creative* force in our lives. Who is at the helm of this powerful force? You can be. Let's begin by lifting the curtain on the surface of the mind and seeing what lies below.

PART
I

The Secrets of
the Mind

The mind, as invisible as it seems, is quite powerful. It is clearly something other than what we usually think of it. How can it be that the window through which we look out onto life, the human mind, is actually a light shining a mysterious image onto the stage we call life? How can it be that life is but a dream? How can the mind possess the amazing qualities suggested by Cayce's psychic trance state? To answer these questions, we need to explore the secrets of the mind.

To do so, we'll begin by looking at some of the common mysteries of the mind. We'll make some of these mysteries seem less strange. We'll learn about our silent partner, the subconscious mind. This hidden genie, just outside our awareness, has some amazing abilities.

If you have ever wondered about ESP, you'll be interested to learn about how the subconscious mind picks up telepathic impressions. Cayce has a surprise in store for us as we explore the meaning of telepathy. One of the secrets of the mind is that it doesn't actually exist where you might expect it to be. As Cayce explains the nature of telepathy, we learn that the mind exists not in your brain, but in a fourth-dimensional world of its own. What you consider to be "your mind" is but a small representative of the whole mind, which is infinite in scope.

You have access to the infinite mind through ideas. Ideas are simultaneously everywhere and always, not just when and where you think them. As we explore the meaning of this unusual perspective, we find that Cayce turns reality on its head. As he does so, he puts the mind within a cosmic and spiritual perspective. You will learn that one of the most important secrets of the mind is that it is a dimension of soul. Cayce explains how the soul projects its reality through the use of the mind and he gives us a formula for creation of reality. We'll learn just exactly how it can be that what we experience in life is a dream of the soul.

Understanding Cayce's metaphysical perspective on the mind will prepare you for a new experiment in living. What you learn here will help you to appreciate the dynamic power behind the practical advice Cayce presents on using the mind's hidden powers to create for yourself an ideal life. That the mind is the way to achieve a better and more meaningful life is truly its greatest secret.

2

The Subconscious:
Hidden Genie of
the Mind

*The study from the human standpoint, of subconscious,
subliminal, psychic, soul forces, is and should
be the great study for the human family, for
through self man will understand its Maker when it
understands its relation to its Maker, and it will
only understand that through itself, and that
understanding is the knowledge as is given
here in this state.*

Edgar Cayce 3744-4

Isn't the mind what we experience it to be? It's only natural
to assume so. The mind is simply there, a living mirror of
who we are and of the world around us. Sometimes,
however, we may suspect that some part of the mind must
be outside of our awareness. Who drove the car while we
were daydreaming? Where do our hunches come from?

Terms like "subconscious" or "unconscious" are quite
familiar today. We have all heard of Freud and psychoanalysis. But the subconscious that Freud made famous has a

reputation as some dark and dismal region, better left alone.

"Who knows what dark and evil secrets lurk in the hearts of men? The Shadow knows!" We'd rather not know what the Shadow knows. That seems to be the general attitude toward the subconscious mind.

Let's shine a new light beneath the surface of the mind. The unconscious has received some bad press. Let's take a different look. Stories of the monsters of the deep won't frighten us away if we can learn to explore the depths of the mind and discover the wonderful resources waiting there.

Dipping Into the Stream of Consciousness

Is your mind out of your control? The idea is offensive. No one likes to think that they have lost control of their mind. A mind out of control means a person has gone crazy. You probably assume that you have control over your mind.

When we say we are "of two minds," it usually means that we think about something in more than one way. We have mixed feelings. That may be our attitude about the unconscious. It may have some tremendous riches for us, but it also implies that we are not always in control of our mind. There are parts of our mind that may control us. Yet we need to get past this barrier.

Let's dip into the subconscious a bit and see what it is like. I have an experiment for you to try. Afterward, you will recognize that I am showing you a familiar, but not always understood, side of your mind.

Let's assume you are in control of your mind. You should be able to decide what it thinks about. So pick something, anything, to think about. Why not make it easy—pick a single word, or a mental picture. Pick something simple to focus on.

Now begin concentrating on that one thing. Close your eyes and say to yourself that one word over and over, again and again. Hold in your mind that mental picture and focus on it. Don't think any other thoughts or imagine any other pictures. Just keep your concentration on that one thing. OK, stop reading for a moment and try it. Try it for maybe thirty seconds ... So what happened? Were you able to maintain your concentration without interruptions? Or did other thoughts and images appear? Did your mind wander? If you are like most people, you found that your mind has a life of its own. There is a stream of thought. You find yourself thinking many other thoughts besides the one you wanted to focus on. If you think that you just got bored, that you could do the experiment if you really wanted to, prove it! Try it again. Otherwise, you'll have to admit, your mind is less under your control than you suspected.

Have you ever had moments when you wanted to control your mind but couldn't? Sometimes it's hard to go to sleep at night because the mind is racing with thoughts. At other times, we think thoughts we'd rather not think. Sometimes we can't locate our thoughts, or can't recall something we want to remember.

You may have also had moments when your mind was working quite well and without any help from you. Thoughts and ideas flowed freely. Perhaps you were having a good talk with a friend about some important topic. You found yourself saying all sorts of wise or thoughtful things that you didn't realize you knew. You didn't have to work to think up what to say, because the thoughts just came to you. It was like being inspired.

The better acquainted you become with your mind, the more you realize that it isn't something that you control in the usual manner. The mind may be a tool to use, but that doesn't mean it sits idle when you are not using it. Although you can learn to direct it, the mind has a "mind of its own." It certainly isn't just a passive mirror, waiting to reflect what comes in front of it. It has its own, active, full life. It has more of a life than you realize.

This stream of thought that you experienced is coming from your subconscious. Although you didn't consciously *decide* to think them, you probably recognized many of these thoughts. They didn't seem strange. As you became aware of them, they felt like they were your own thoughts. They were you thinking of other things. These were the thoughts that were "on your mind," so to speak. You see, there is more depth to you than simply the surface of your mind. Behind that surface are background thoughts, images, and feelings. If all these thoughts came to the surface at the same time, they would confuse you. That's where the subconscious helps out.

The very top surface of the subconscious mind is like a valet or assistant. It prepares your thoughts, holds them at the ready, and lets you choose among them. When you confront a situation, your subconscious immediately gathers many thoughts and has them ready for you. It allows you to think only a couple of thoughts at a time, at your choosing. Probably you are already familiar with this part of the subconscious mind, although you may not have called it by name. It is not at all unfriendly, and actually quite helpful.

Consciousness, or thinking, is like a stream. The water flows at many depths. With our attention, we dip into this stream, and bring to the surface what we need at the moment. We don't control this stream in the sense of being able to turn it off or on. Nor do we directly control what flows through it. Yet we have some say in what we attend to and what we bring to the surface. There is much beneath the surface that we could use, if we knew how to dip that deeply.

The conscious mind is narrow and fragile compared to the depths and power of the subconscious. The subconscious is an ally. It is like having a superman or wonderwoman at our side ready to assist us. Although hidden, it is truly a genie. Let's examine some of its spectacular abilities.

The Subliminal Power of the Subconscious

The conscious mind is like a focused light. It shines very brightly, but only upon a limited spot. What it gains by being able to concentrate intently, it looses in other capacities. While the direction of your attention focuses your conscious mind, your subconscious mind has a diffuse awareness in all directions. It is as supersensitive as the latest radar equipment.

Nothing escapes the notice of the subconscious mind. While you are paying attention to a task, it is quietly absorbing much information around you. It is much like a dog or cat that sits by your side, guarding you. It allows you to go about your business without your having to monitor events around you. It knows the difference between normally occurring events and unexpected ones. While you read this book, for example, you are almost deaf to the various noises happening in your environment. Should a strange noise occur, your subconscious immediately alerts you and cocks your ears.

You can tell that your subconscious mind pays more attention than you do when someone unexpectedly speaks to you. You may instinctively respond by saying, "Huh?" You weren't paying attention when the person started to speak, so you assumed you didn't hear them. Almost before they can repeat themselves, however, your subconscious mind repeats the statement for you. You can hear in your mind a tape-recorded playback of their words. It's like a tape recording because you can even hear the tone of the person's voice. Your subconscious mind registered perfectly the event even though you weren't paying attention.

The subconscious mind is so sensitive it can perceive things your conscious mind would consider impossible to notice. It has almost unlimited powers of perception. You could say it had "bionic senses," a sensory system technologically advanced beyond normal human abilities.

You may have heard about subliminal advertising. You may have seen ads for subliminal tapes that deliver suggestions to your subconscious mind. We'll look at the suggestion angle later in this book. For the moment, however, let's focus on the power of your subconscious mind to simply perceive subliminal stimulation that escapes your awareness. Just how sensitive the subconscious can be will surprise you.

Subliminal stimulation can happen in a variety of ways. It can flash before your eyes. It can be a whisper of sound. It can come as a touch, a smell, or a taste. In fact, it can come through intuitions, too. We receive a lot of telepathic information in a subliminal fashion. All that "subliminal" means is that the information does not register in the conscious mind.

Using sensitive microelectrodes to record brain activity, scientists can determine when the brain registers sensations. Researchers have found that the brain detects touches to the body that are so slight that the person notices nothing. The same is true for visual stimulation. The brain sees more than the person notices. Furthermore, such brain-recording experiments have shown that the brain not only detects the stimulation, but also analyzes its meaning. The subconscious mind perceives things and understands their significance while the conscious mind remains totally oblivious.

Consider this situation: You are listening to some instrumental music. You hear nothing unusual. However, there is actually a verbal message recorded in with the music. The message is so soft that you cannot hear it. A person's voice says, "You are walking up an endless flight of stairs." Although you are unaware of any message, your subconscious mind hears the message. How do we know? Experiments have shown that the message affects how you respond to the music.

If you daydream to the music, or simply list words the music suggests to you, your thoughts will show hints of the message. Compared to people listening to the same music without any subliminal message, your associations will contain more references to topics related to walking up stairs. Your daydream will contain more ideas about making an effort, exertion, being tired, walking, exploring, climbing, achieving, and related topics. Your subconscious mind perceived the contents of the subliminal message as if it were a part of the music.

The subliminal effect also works even if you can consciously detect the presence of the subliminal stimulus. Re-recording the verbal message at a higher speed again and again reduces it to squeak. When that little squeak is added into the recording of the music, you can hear it. It almost sounds like another note, although out of place. Afterward, your daydream about the music will again show the effect of the subliminal message. It was just a pip of a squeak to your conscious mind, but was a fully deciperable message to your subconscious mind.

Think about it for a moment. Think what these experiments show about the perceptive power of the subconscious mind.

The subliminal power of your subconscious mind extends to the sense of smell, too. You react to odors that your conscious mind doesn't even notice. Cayce noted, in fact, that odors have a more powerful effect upon us than any other sensory stimuli. Most of these effects are subliminal. Scientists have just begun to measure the effects of such invisible odors.

Women's menstrual cycles, for example, are sensitive to

the odors of other women. When women are together for a long time, their periods become synchronized. Researchers have collected armpit odors from women with regular periods and applied them to women with irregular periods. As these women wear these odors, their periods become regular.

Scientists in England have placed male armpit odors, without noticeable scent, on the doors to public toilets. Men, but not women, avoided those toilets. The experimenters speculated that men apparently preferred toilets that give no indication that another man was recently there. A subconscious reaction to a subliminal odor revealed the men's territorial behavior. Animal instincts die hard.

We think we have only five senses. The subconscious has at least a sixth sense. It responds to electromagnetism. The ability to dowse for water comes from the response to subliminal electromagnetic stimulation. It also helps us in our sense of direction. One researcher drove blindfolded schoolchildren far from home, and then asked them to point to the way back. They were able to do so. In another experiment, however, the blindfolds contained magnets. The magnets confused the children's sense of orientation and they were unable to point to the way home. The subconscious probably contains other senses that await discovery.

The sensitivity of the subconscious mind seems to have no bounds. It is so sensitive, in fact, that it registers when someone is just *thinking* about us. There's truth to the saying that if your ears are burning, someone is talking about you. The subliminal powers of the subconscious mind extend to ESP. We'll learn more about that later.

Try to create an image for yourself of your subconscious mind. Visualize it as an ultrasensitive receiver of information. How would you picture it? You might see it as a network of antennae that surround your body. Or you might see it as a set of invisible eyes, ears, nose, etc., but much larger than your physical sensory tools. Develop a positive image of the subconscious mind so that you may feel more friendly toward it.

The Perfect Memory of the Subconscious

Not only is the subconscious extremely perceptive, it has the memory of an elephant. You've probably heard about the use of hypnosis to retrieve long-lost memories. Recent court decisions have recognized the legitimacy of hypnosis as a means of enhancing the memory of witnesses to crimes. People see a lot more than they notice or can remember, but the subconscious notices and remembers. Using hypnosis, a person can mentally replay the past with such accurate vividness that one can describe previously disregarded details.

Under hypnosis people have gone back to early-childhood experiences and relived them in surprising detail. In one study, for example, hypnotized adults regressed back to their tenth, seventh, and fourth birthdays. They described the events of each of these days. They also answered a test question about the day of the week of that birthday. Calendar checks proved the accuracy of their recall. The accuracy rate was 93 percent for the day of their tenth birthday. It was 82 percent for their seventh birthday and 69 percent for their fourth birthday. A four-year-old child might only be subliminally aware of the day of the week. Years later, however, the subconscious mind still has an accurate memory for the day.

Dreams are a common place to discover the perfect memory of the subconscious. That's how I first experienced it for myself. I dreamed of a young girl celebrating her tenth birthday. She was running with her friends while carrying a bottle of champagne. She dropped the bottle and the champagne came pouring out. She was upset, and I rushed to her aid. I bent down to rescue the bottle from emptying itself. I hesitated, however, and watched the last bit of sparkling yellow fluid drain from the bottle.

At the time of the dream, I was a newly recovering alcoholic. I saw my action in the dream reflecting my decision to let alcoholic beverages vacate completely from my life. Someone asked me what ten-year anniversary I was celebrating. I wasn't aware that I was experiencing any such anniversary. I checked the calendar, went back ten years, and searched through what records I had kept. It amazed me to discover that it was the ten-year anniversary of my first drink! The dream was marking the anniversary of that event. My subconscious had remembered the date. It indirectly referred to it in my dream to make a comment on my decision to stop drinking.

Dreams are a frequent source of subconscious memories. By contemplating the feelings in a dream, you will quite likely recall a surprising early-childhood memory. The memory will also contain the feelings of that early experience. Research has shown the effectiveness of this technique. It is something you can experiment with yourself. How much your subconscious remembers will surprise you.

The subconscious even remembers subliminal experiences. It registers and retains childhood events, for example, that the child does not consciously perceive. These subliminal experiences affect the child's behavior into adulthood.

Such invisible memories appear sometimes in dreams. It is almost impossible, however, for us to detect them there. We are not even aware of originally having the experience in the first place. We cannot recognize the experience as a memory. It is primarily from the work of psychotherapists that we know dreams can bring up subliminal memories from childhood.

I once read the case study of a woman who was seeking treatment for bulimia, the gorge-purge eating disorder. She had a dream that suggested to her therapist that she had subconsciously perceived a dangerous secret when she was an infant. It was that her father was having an affair with another woman. The patient said that she knew that the therapist was wrong. She spoke with her mother, who assured her that there had been no affair.

At the therapist's urging, the woman contacted her father. She asked him about it. He reluctantly confided that there had been an affair, but that no one, including her mother, had ever known about. He asked her to please keep it a secret. The revelation came as a terrible shock to the woman.

With the therapist's help, she realized she had an unconscious tendency to protect her mother from having bad feelings. She would try to absorb these feelings herself. This habit had begun in infancy, when she had unconsciously sensed the father's secret and its implications for her mother. When the father asked her, as an adult, not to reveal the secret, the pattern became obvious. The revelation proved to mark the turning point in the therapy. The woman was able to unburden herself of feelings that were not truly her own, but which really belonged to her parents. When she stopped absorbing their feelings, she no longer needed to purge herself.

Her dream had dredged up a crucial secret. It concerned something that as an infant she could have sensed only subliminally.

This story shows that the subconscious is able to search for an important buried memory that only it knows exists. Not only is its memory perfect, but it shows intelligent use of its memory. It recognizes critical moments in our lives when certain memories would be useful. It finds them and brings them to light.

The Creativity of the Subconscious

The subconscious does more than simply register and retain information. It is also able to operate on this information. It can think creatively. It can analyze information to detect patterns the conscious mind fails to notice.

One of the places that reveals the creativity of the subconscious is our dreams. Consider, for example, this puzzle: Here are five letters, O,T,T,F,F. What two letters do you think would come next? If you can't figure out the answer, you are not alone. Stanford University students were unable to solve it. Then they tried to "sleep on it" to see if their dreams might solve the puzzle.

Some of the students were indeed able to solve the puzzle in their sleep. The researcher, Dr. William Dement, reported one of the dreams. A student dreamed of being in an art gallery looking at a row of paintings on the wall. He began to count them. He counted one, two, three, four, five pictures, then saw that the next two frames were empty. He then realized that the numbers six and seven were the answers to the puzzle.

The subconscious noticed the subliminal message in the letters. They were the first letters of the numbers, one through five.

In another experiment, a professor of mathematics tested his ability to solve calculus problems. The experimenter then hypnotized the professor. He gave him a posthypnotic suggestion that he could solve calculus problems rapidly in his head. The professor then did so. Rather than using a pencil to work out the answers, he worked them out mentally. His speed and accuracy improved significantly over the first testing. He claimed that he could skip steps and the answers just came to him.

The subconscious mind can also stop the clock to gain more time to solve problems. In one demonstration, a hypnotized dress designer followed suggestions to slow time to a standstill. The hypnotists suggested to her that the next ten seconds would seem like an hour. During that hypnotic hour, she was to design a new dress. Ten seconds later, she awakened and drew her new design. She was very happy with the results. She said that to create such a new design she would have needed at least an hour! Her subconscious had provided it in ten seconds.

Relative to the conscious mind, the subconscious mind may appear like a genius. The subconscious has the reputation of being something that is a disturbance to the conscious mind. But it is really the reverse: the conscious mind tramples on the subconscious and holds it back. When the conscious mind can get out of the way, the subconscious can show its talent.

There is a mental abnormality called the "idiot savant" syndrome. The conscious mind is severely retarded, but there are signs of a creative genius. A person with this malady has some remarkable ability. Someone who doesn't know how to read or write can nevertheless perform amazing feats of mental arithmetic. Mentally multiplying 8,356,356 by 356,453 requires only seconds. Someone with no musical training is nevertheless able to listen to a complex classical piano solo and then replay it perfectly. Some are able to compose new music or create beautiful drawings. Idiot savants reveal that hidden in the subconscious mind is a genius waiting to awaken.

The Subconscious Mind in Daily Life

One of the main jobs of the subconscious, to which Cayce pointed our attention, is the monitoring of actions that have become habitual. When we first learn a skill, such as tying our shoes, riding a bicycle, typing, or driving a car, it requires all of our attention. Once we have mastered it, we pay it little attention. The subconscious takes over and carries out the task for us. Only when some unexpected, nonroutine event occurs does the subconscious call our attention to the task at hand. Perhaps you have noticed that sort of thing while driving. You didn't realize you were daydreaming until you were suddenly pressing on the brakes. The subconscious had alerted you to come back.

The subconscious mind is also a faithful, behind-the-scene servant in most of our mental operations. When we talk with someone, we are able to speak in an unending flow of words. We don't have to pause after each phrase in order to think up the next phrase. Our subconscious mind gathers thoughts for us in large groups, then presents them to us as we need to speak them.

When we listen to someone else speak, we can only hold about seven words in mind at one time. Yet we don't have to ask the person to pause every few words. Our subconscious remembers all the words and helps us understand what the person is saying.

While we are listening to the other person, our subconscious mind is also gathering replies for us. It has them at the ready when it is our turn to speak. Sometimes you notice this process in action. When you do, however, it is harder for you to listen to what the other person is saying. At such times, it is better to let the subconscious do its work unnoticed. Otherwise, we defeat its purpose.

The subsconscious mind also controls the operations of our body. Cayce noted how the subconscious monitors our bodily functions and keeps them running smoothly. You didn't think, did you, that the body ran without an intelligence directing it? Who keeps your heart beating, regulates its speed so it goes faster when necessary, or slows it down when you are resting? Your subconscious mind. It also regulates the digestive process. It slows it down, for example, when you decide you're going to work immediately after a meal rather than rest. The various bodily functions work together, changing as needed to differing circumstances. The subconscious mind is the conductor of this harmonic symphony.

Neurophysiology has come to understand how the bloodstream and the nervous system network the body's various organs. The final master of this network of organization is deep in the brain, according to standard textbook physiology. Cayce noted, however, that it is the subconscious mind that is using the brain as a tool in its efforts.

The brain is *not* the mind! Instead, the mind uses the brain as a tool. In fact, the subconscious mind uses every atom in the body in its expression. Every atom in the body has its portion of mind. Being "of one mind," as in single-purposed, means having every atom in the body acting in harmony.

Cayce anticipated psychically what modern neurophysiology would later learn through laboratory research. By learning to make contact with the subconscious mind, we can ourselves direct the functioning of the body. Experiments have shown that this control extends to single nerve cells and to individual blood cells. In the future, science will have the means to observe this control extending to the atomic level of the body.

The Nature of the Subconscious Mind

When giving readings on the nature of the subconscious mind, Cayce often recommended that we read Thomson Jay Hudson's book *The Law of Psychic Phenomena* for more information. Although written in 1892, it continues to be a

valuable textbook on the nature of the subconscious mind.
Here we will mention but a few of the attributes of this
hidden genie, suggesting that you, too, read Hudson's book
for more information.

The subconscious mind is subjective, while the conscious
mind is objective. Our conscious mind focuses on external
appearances. Its world is the "objective reality" of the
senses. The subconscious mind accepts internal appearances. What seems true for us from a subjective viewpoint
is reality to the subconscious. While objective reality seems
to be the master of the conscious mind, the subconscious is
the servant of our subjective reality.

While the conscious mind relies on the senses and reasons
logically, the subconscious operates on the principle of
suggestion. When we talk to ourselves, the subconscious
listens and accepts what we say to ourselves as true. When
untended, this power of suggestion can work against us. Our
subconscious registers the negative things we think about
ourselves and accepts them as reality. The reverse is also
true. It accepts our wishes and hopes as facts and can help
bring them about. That's why it is worthwhile for us to
harness the power of suggestion and use it to our benefit.

The use of pictures, or imagery, is another example of the
subjectivity of the subconscious mind. It uses a picture
language to do its thinking. In one experiment, for example,
a hypnotized subject listened to a series of numbers and
made up a dream about them. The experimenter read them
aloud at a normal speed: 6, 5, 3, 9, 8, 8, 0, 1. Immediately
afterward, the person reported the dream. It was of a curved
pipe (shaped like the number 6), with a five-pointed star in
the bowl. The man breaks the pipe in half, because half of
six is three. He then turns it upside down to make a golf
club (a nine iron). He sees two symbols for infinity (figure
eights), and announces that all is nothing (0): it's all the
same one thing (1). The subject was able to repeat back

the numbers perfectly. The experiment shows how quickly the subconscious can turn facts into images.

The subconscious mind also thinks symbolically. The conscious mind thinks in a literal fashion, responding to the factual meaning of words. The subconscious responds to the emotional meanings of words, and gives free rein to its imagination. Symbols are not true to literal facts. Instead, they express feelings and subjective appearances. The symbolic logic of the subconscious is what gives rise to dreams, myths, and fairy tales. These stories, although not factually accurate, speak of truths of the soul.

For example, while the conscious mind sees no immediate relationship between a turtle and the planet earth, to the subconscious mind they are very similar. The curves on the turtle's shell is like the surface of the planet, with its bumps and valleys. The planet is a home that travels, just like the turtle carries its home on its back. There is an American Indian legend that reflects these symbolic parallels. According to this legend, the origin of the earth was the back of a giant turtle. The legend wisely speaks of the importance of a certain quality, both shy and modest yet strong and patient, that is necessary to sustain life on earth.

Because of the free play it gives to the imagination, the subconscious sees multifaceted, quaint connections that go beyond strict logic. It can also show as much insight as an ancient sage. Although it doesn't seem realistic or objective, it is nevertheless intelligent. Although innocent and gullible in its unquestioning acceptance of suggestions, it can be very wise.

Speaking symbolically, the conscious mind is like the sun while the subconscious is like the moon. The sun's bright light reveals details to our eyes. The diffuse light of the moon arouses our feelings. When the sun shines brightly during the day, lighting up the sky, the moon is barely visible. At night, when the sun has left the sky dark, the moon shines brightly. The workings of the subconscious also appear more readily when the conscious mind relaxes or sleeps. The sun's role in the life of the planet is obvious. Yet the moon also has powerful effects. It is smaller than the sun, but closer to the earth. Its gravitational force affects the tides, the growth of plants, and the fluids in our own bodies. The moon may not give off its own light, but its energies nevertheless affect us. In the bright light of day, our conscious mind operates through the senses and the intellect, two sharply focused powers. The moonlight gives the subconscious mind the quiet stealth of intuition. It uses the subtle play of feelings to help it reveal an equally important reality.

The conscious mind is also symbolized by a man. The male often thinks itself the ruler and the wisest of all. The subconscious is symbolized as a woman. She has a quiet wisdom of her own that often confounds the man's more focused, linear intelligence. As we appreciate the special wisdom and intelligence of the feminine perspective, we realize the special value of the subconscious mind.

This hidden genie, the subconscious mind, a servant and guardian with bionic sensitivity and creative vision, deserves our respect. As we attend to its subtle promptings, it can lead us toward still more mysteries of the mind.

3

ESP and
the Transpersonal Mind

Mind, then, may function without a form or body.
                                        Edgar Cayce 262-78

Each of us is a separate person. We each have our own mind. That seems pretty obvious.

Our skin defines the boundaries of who we are. Our separate brains operate separate minds. Your mind stays inside your head, while my mind keeps its place inside my head.

Each of us is obviously separate from the environment, from the world. We're not glued to it. We're free to walk about freely while the world holds still. The world doesn't move with every step we take. The rest of life passes by while we watch. We don't move with it. We each lead our own lives, separate from the world.

It's also clear that what's inside our minds is something different from the stuff that's "out there" in the world. You can touch things, but how do you touch your mind? It's "stuff" that makes the world matter. It's the concrete reality of chemistry and physics. The body and the brain is part of this physical world, but what about the mind? The mind is somehow different. It's made of something else—thoughts and images.

All this is obvious. So what? It seems so obvious, but it's just not true. It's only a working convenience the conscious mind uses. The separation, between ourselves and others and between inside and outside, is the creation of the conscious mind. It is its most significant achievement and its major curse.

To avoid this curse, we'll need to see beyond the illusion of the conscious mind. To use the mind to its fullest creativity, we must introduce the conscious mind to its source—the transpersonal mind. It is not an easy task.

Subliminal ESP Powers of the Subconscious Mind

Our conscious mind may accept the idea of an unconscious. When it does, however, it typically puts a limit on it. Our normal conception of the unconscious is like a pocket, a hidden drawer, or the cellar of our house. It is a container, a place to put memories.

We have already seen that part of the unconscious, the subconscious, is more than just a pocket. It is an active power and extremely perceptive. It is not a container at all, nor is it bounded or contained. In fact, it may have no walls. Besides being our secret servant, it also has invisible connections with other subconscious minds.

When we are with others, for example, our conscious mind can create for us the lonely feeling of "self-consciousness." We peer out from behind our eyes across the crowded room and sense other people peering out from their eyes at us. We become the objects of their seeing as they are the objects of ours. The conscious mind creates impressions of separateness.

The subconscious mind experiences the situation in a

different way. It is very sensitive to the emotional atmosphere in the room. These vibrations are the reality for the subconscious. It is something the subconscious intuitively feels even if there are no sensory cues that the conscious mind can perceive. We can feel one another's feelings almost as if there were a connection between us.

Our conscious mind rejects such thoughts. That is, unless it has studied the evidence for telepathy. Nevertheless, our conscious mind sometimes feels uncomfortable focusing on such feelings. The subconscious, however, cannot ignore them.

I'm sure that you have had such an experience yourself in a room of people. Perhaps you wanted to ignore the impression you were picking up. You didn't know if you could trust it, and you didn't know what to do with it. Nevertheless, it probably affected how you approached the situation in the room.

The subliminal ESP powers of the subconscious mind influence your thoughts, feelings, and actions. Your conscious mind is not aware of this influence, but it exists. Research has repeatedly demonstrated that the subconscious mind detects other people's thoughts.

Douglas Dean of the Newark College of Engineering devised this test of subliminal ESP. The subject provides the researcher with ten names of people who are emotionally important in the person's life. The researcher adds ten additional names randomly chosen from the phone book and copies all twenty onto individual cards. The researcher goes into another room and hands all the cards to another person. This person silently reads each name while the researcher records the subject's reaction on a plethysomgraph. This machine records blood flow in a fingertip and detects minute changes in the person's emotional state.

When the sender reads a name known to the subject, the subject's blood flow shows a response. Somehow the subject knows when the sender is thinking about someone of significance. Consciously, however, the subject doesn't experience anything in particular. Just sitting there quietly, the subject isn't even aware of the nature of the experiment. The subconscious, however, and the body it controls, show uncanny sensitivity.

Other experiments have demonstrated that other people's experiences affect the contents of our thoughts through subliminal ESP. Dr. Thelma Moss from UCLA's medical school, for example, showed that what one person concentrates on can leak into the daydreams of another person in a nearby room. Dr. Montague Ullman and his colleagues at the Maimonides Hospital in Brooklyn found that a sleeping person can pick up on the thoughts of other people and weave them into dreams.

We are not usually aware that telepathy is influencing our mind. Evidence of a subliminal ESP effect is quite clear to the observing researcher, however. In the experiment just mentioned, people contemplated colorful pictures. Images from these pictures made obvious appearances in the dreams and daydreams of the experimental subjects. The subjects assumed that their thoughts were their own. The researchers knew otherwise.

These scientific findings are but a few examples of what Cayce meant by the connection between subconscious minds. Your subconscious mind is in contact with all other subconscious minds. It is not only Santa Claus who knows what we have been thinking! Everyone has access to everyone else's thoughts. Even if we are not consciously aware of what others are thinking, their thoughts nevertheless affect us.

The Unconscious Connection

What are we to make of the subconscious mind if we are to accept that it has no boundaries? Isn't our mind our own?

I know I experience my own mind as something that floats inside my head. I don't normally experience it as extending outside of me to be in direct contact with other minds. Although I can appreciate the evidence for subliminal ESP, it's still hard for me to visualize the connection between minds.

Edgar Cayce gave a pictorial model of the link between minds. What his model shows is stranger than fiction. It shows there is one mind and people share it. The drawing in Figure 1 is Cayce's image of the mind.

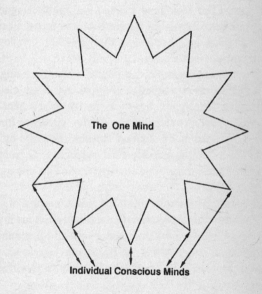

Figure 1

The Relation between Individual
Conscious Minds and the One Mind

The drawing is of a multipointed star. The star itself represents the entire mind. Each arm of the star represents a portion of the mind for a different person. To be more accurate, we would need a star with billions of points, but what we have will do. The very tip of each point represents the conscious mind of an individual.

The mind you usually think of as "your mind" is but one of the points on the star. It is your conscious mind. Our conscious minds are only a very, very small portion of the entire mind. If you value you conscious mind, and I trust that you do, then look how much more mind there is to value! Our conscious minds are quite wondrous themselves. So imagine the wonder of the whole mind!

The appearance of conscious minds is the result of the growth of the star. Beginning as a round shape, it developed arms that grew to very sharp points. A conscious mind is capable of very exact, penetrating focus. Yet it also becomes isolated from the rest of the mind by this very narrow focus. As one point on the star appears distinct from the others, one conscious mind seems separate and distant from other conscious minds.

Looking out upon the world with the eyes of our conscious mind, we see through our own point on the star. The conscious mind operates through its sensitivity to physical sensations. When we look out upon the world through our hearts, we use the intuitive ability of the subconscious. Through the unconscious we make connections through the inner part of the star.

In Figure 2, we see how the unconscious mind is a continuous connective layer of the inner parts of the mind's arms. The star tips only seem separate from one another. The arms of the stars are clearly like fingers on the same hand. The arms represent our subconscious minds. All subconscious minds are connected. The core of the mind is available to us all, via what Cayce termed the superconscious mind.

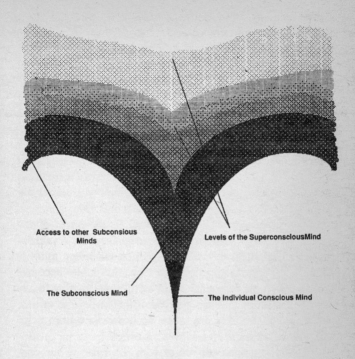

Access to other Subconsious
Minds

Levels of the SuperconsciousMind

The Subconscious Mind

The Individual Conscious Mind

Figure 2

Regions of the Mind

An Experiment in Telepathy

With our conscious mind, we cannot make contact with
any other point on the star except by way of sensory

contact. You can't talk to anyone who is not present with
you, except by aid of a telephone to bridge the gap. To
"reach out and touch someone" with the conscious mind,
you need a special tool. All of our senses are special tools for
detecting physical energy. The communication devices that
we have developed are tools to extend the range of the senses.

Only the conscious mind needs such tools. With the
subconscious mind, we can directly reach out to someone
with our feelings. How else to explain that phone call from
a friend you were just thinking about?

On the basis of this common experience, in fact, Cayce
indicates that you can learn for yourself the secret of
telepathy. He suggests that you conduct this simple experiment. Make an agreement with a friend to stop what you are
doing at the same time every day and tune in to each other.

Simply focus on that feeling of your subconscious connection with that person. What does it feel like to be in the
presence of that person? That is the "wavelength," as it
were, to attune to. Then let your thoughts, images, and
daydreams have a free run. Note what passes through your
mind. Arrange to speak with your friend, over the phone
perhaps, every few days to compare notes. Chances are very
good that you and your friend will find that each of you
experienced thoughts and images that correspond with events
in the other person's life.

Other people have tried this experiment with good results.
The author Upton Sinclair described the good results he had
with his wife in his book *Mental Radio*. The psychic Harold
Sherman described in *Thoughts Through Space* use of this
method to track Sir Hubert Wilkins on his expedition to the
South Pole. Most recently, researchers Russell Targ and
Harold Putoff reported in their book *Mind Race* the results
of their experiments showing that anyone can do this type of
telepathy, which they call "remote viewing."

You may have had other experiences besides this form of

telepathy that suggest to you the connection between subconscious minds. You can learn more about Cayce's view on
the development of telepathy and other forms of psychic
awareness in my book *Awakening Your Psychic Powers*.

Certainly, not all ESP is subliminal. Furthermore, as the
center of Cayce's star model suggests, our connection with
one another goes deeper than the subconscious.

Archetypes:
Pictures From the Universal Unconscious

While making his rounds of the psychiatric hospital, Dr.
Carl Jung was approached by an excited patient. He asked
the good doctor to please come to the window. He wanted
Jung to look up in the sky at the sun. "See, the sun is
wagging its tail!" exclaimed the man. "It is making the
wind!"

Some time later, Dr. Jung had reason to marvel at the
patient's hallucination. It wasn't that the person could see
something that was not there. Hallucinations were common-
place in the hospital.

It was something that Jung later discovered, when reading
a translation, for the first time in German, of an obscure
Greek text over two thousand years old. The text concerned
an initiation ceremony into a religious cult. During the
ceremony, the initiate experiences a secret revelation of the
sun's tail and learns that it is what makes the wind. The
details of this long-obscure religious ceremony were remark-
ably similar to the patient's hallucination.

How could the imagination of this poor, uneducated
peasant parallel so exactly an obscure myth from an ancient
culture? How could he have heard of it? That was the
marvel. There seemed to be no way that it was possible.

This incident led Jung, a Swiss psychiatrist and a contem-

porary of Sigmund Freud, to research the deepest depths of
the mind. He found himself in search of the source of
universal symbolism. He found evidence of such symbolism
not only in the hallucinations of the mentally ill but also in
the dreams of ordinary people. He found it in the religions
of the world, as well as in myths and fairy tales of all ages.

Cultural heritage or learning cannot explain the appearance of these common symbols. They are innate, arising
directly from a universal level of the mind.

It was this discovery that forced Jung to develop a branch
of psychoanalysis distinct from that created by Freud. When
Freud discovered the unconscious, he thought he had found
a pocket of repressed memories and urges. It was his theory
of the unconscious that influenced our envisioning it like a
cellar. Jung, however, found that the unconscious is more
like a spring from a vast underground reservoir.

Jung noted, for example, that patients who had recovered
all their repressed memories through years of psychoanalysis nevertheless continued to bring up fresh material from
the unconscious. The unconscious doesn't run dry, but flows
from an infinite source.

Jung proposed a psychoanalytic theory based on what he
called the archetypes of a universal unconscious. These
archetypes are a set of universal patterns from which all
symbols evolve. They point to a region of the mind that
exists as a common link between all people, living and dead.

Each person's mind, regardless of what it has, or has not,
taken in through learning, shows evidence of having deep
roots into a universal mind. From these roots, ancient
symbols spontaneously arise into the minds of unsuspecting
individuals. These symbols represent ideas that the person
has never consciously experienced. They do not result from
learning or experience. They reflect instead an archetypal
thought pattern that is innate to the mind itself.

Let's look at one example, from the case records of

psychiatrist Dr. Edward Whitmont, as he presented it in his book *The Symbolic Quest.*

There was a young child with asthma who had a recurrent dream. It was about trying to climb out of the water onto the dry land of an island. A great "goat man" was always pushing her back into the water. From the dream we might suppose that her growth was being somehow suppressed. Her asthma was the result of some type of drowning. But by what force?

When Dr. Whitmont interviewed the mother, he learned that she, too, had a recurrent dream. It was that an Eastern potentate was trying to break into her house. He threatened that if she did not let him in, he would kill the child.

Dr. Whitmont recognized that both dreams were referring to the Eastern goat god, Ammon, worshipped by Egyptians two thousand years before Christ. This deity relates to the earthy instincts of natural life. It is the same energy that the Christian church later rejected as the horned "devil."

The devil that was drowning the child, however, was not the Christian devil. It was the devil of the mother's rigid attitude. She denied the instinctual, spontaneous, joyous, and sensual side of life in favor of rigid opinions. Even though the mother verbally expressed a liberal attitude, her emotional stance toward her child was quite controlling. She always knew best where her daughter was concerned.

The daughter didn't even have room to breathe. Her mother's anxiety concerning the basic life energies made it impossible for the child to gain a handle on them for herself. When the mother was able to "loosen up," the child could literally "breathe easier."

The two dreams go together hand in glove. Their similarity shows the subconscious connection between mother and child.

The child's dream also shows that she had an unconscious

understanding of what was happening to her. The symbol of
the goat man, however, was not part of the child's own
language or experience. It reflected the recognition by the
archetypal unconscious of the source of the girl's difficulty.
It expressed this understanding using an image four thousand years old. The archetypal mind produced an image
from an ancient vocabulary and used it appropriately to
diagnose the situation. An ancient and universal awareness
spoke through the child's dream.

The archetypal unconscious is not simply a source of
universal symbols. It also seems to be alert and aware of the
current situation. It speaks in an ancient tongue, but makes
an important point.

Carl Jung, as well as those who have further explored this
area of research, found that this archetypal mind is very
wise. It is as if it were a sage who had lived for thousands
and thousands of years. Yet it keeps up to date on current
events in the lives of people. The main concern of this
ancient sage seems to be a spiritual question: How can the
fullness of God be expressed in the particular life of this
individual?

Can it be that in the depths of your mind, of my mind,
and the mind of every person, there exists the mind of God?
Cayce's source indicated so, and called it the superconscious
mind. It is the infinite mind that exists within all life and
knows no boundaries.

Whereas it is the subconscious mind that handles telepathy, it is through the superconscious mind that clairvoyance
and intuition operate. Edgar Cayce demonstrated a clairvoy-
ant ability in his psychic trance. It is the ability to gather
information at a distance without the intermediary of another mind. Whereas Cayce indicated that he could diagnose
a distant person's illness by telepathically reading the person's own subconscious knowledge of the body's condition,
it was through the superconscious mind that Cayce operated

clairvoyantly. One of these impressive feats was to specify the location of a needed medicine. It was no longer manufactured, but Cayce's clairvoyance impressed upon him the vision of a dusty bottle of this remedy on the back shelf of a particular pharmacy in a distant town. When the pharmacist was called and convinced to look where Cayce had suggested, he indeed found the bottle, hidden behind the current stock.

Our clairvoyance most frequently operates through intuition. Cayce indicated that intuition was the highest form of psychic functioning. Intuitions arise as they are needed, and are meant to guide us. They alert us to opportunities, warn us of dangers, and suggest particular actions. Intuition is a prompter. It is the nudge of the superconscious mind.

It is because of the superconscious mind that Cayce reminded us constantly that all knowledge is within. Although we look outside of ourselves to learn, to gain advice, to obtain assistance, everything that we experience and learn is the result of our inner response. We must learn to look within.

We will learn later about meditation and dreams, two of the places that it is the easiest to begin the process of turning within. We will see how the superconscious mind is the most active when we are asleep and our conscious mind merges with a universal level of awareness. Our dreams are the footprints of intuitive impressions.

The Transpersonal Mind

Jung's discovery of a universal level of the unconscious shared by all people fits with Cayce's model of the mind. There is only one star in that model because there is only one mind. Although the mind may have many points of conscious awareness, as in individual human beings, there is only one mind. In religions and spiritual traditions this mind has gone by several names; the universal mind, the mind at large, or the mind of God.

In the language of today's leading-edge psychology, we would say that the mind is transpersonal. The word *transpersonal* is a recent term invented to express in a new way the same ancient idea whose time has come once again. People from many different branches of science and philosophy have been embracing it, for as many different reasons, since the consciousness revolution of the sixties.

Transpersonal means that the mind has a life beyond what appears in individual persons. The mind is not just what happens inside a person. It is a reality in itself.

The mind is like the air we breathe. Does air exist just when it is in our lungs? Of course not. Does mind exist only when it is active within a brain? It does not, although we usually think of the mind that way.

We could say that you have your air and I have mine. Like the mind, however, air is transpersonal. Air is everywhere. There is one large body of air, but it occupies many different places. Some of it is flowing through my lungs, some of it is flowing through yours. Air threads together all the plants, animals, and people, as well as all the boxes, bottles, homes, and other hollow containers.

Air exists independently of what houses it. The mind exists independently of those who use it. There is only one air. There is only one mind. It is a *single,* living reality.

While it's hard to think of mind as being a single reality, we can think of nature that way. We can picture nature as an impersonal whole and as a law unto itself. We can see nature as a primary reality of its own, even though it has many and various appearances. The reality of nature transcends the specifics of any single piece of nature.

Try thinking of mind in the same way. Imagine the mind as an impersonal whole. Picture it as a world of its own, with its own life, and laws of its own. The life of the mind goes beyond any one individual's experience with it. It exists independently of any living body and continues after the death of that body. The mind is transpersonal.

Ideas: The Fourth Dimension

What is the mind made of that it can exist independently of a living body? Actually, the mind exists independently of more than just a body, but of time and space as well. The mind is of another dimension. According to Cayce, the mind exists in a fourth dimension. It is the world of patterns we usually call ideas.

Where do you go to find ideas? Into your mind, of course. Another name for the mind might be "idealand," or the "ideaosphere." Idealand is a world of its own.

An idea doesn't live in time and space—how long is an idea? How much does it weigh? It's an obvious fact, but often overlooked, that ideas do not have physical properties.

Consider the idea of danger. We know what the idea means, but what physical measurements can you make on it? As an idea, it does not exist in just one place, nor at just one time. Danger is a meaning that is universally experienced by both animals and humans (and perhaps plants, too) throughout history. It is an example of what Jung meant by archetype, because it is a universal pattern of experience. It is an idea rather than any one specific thing or event.

The things that ideas refer to are of this world, but the ideas themselves are not. We can't really measure ideas by a ruler, a bathroom scale, or a clock. We sometimes talk about them as if we could: we "toss ideas around," we "stomp on ideas," we "look for ideas," we "weigh ideas against one another," finding some ideas "more forceful" than others, and we say "an idea's time has come." As someone once said, however, "You can't shoot an idea!" You can burn a book, but not the ideas it contains. An idea is not of this world.

Specific manifestations of an idea may appear at a certain time, or at a certain place, but the ideas themselves live in different kind of reality. The real world of ideas is the world of the mind.

In the time/space world, we understand how one event causes another, as a matter of the law of chemistry and physics. In the reality of the mind, one idea may also invariably lead to another. Yet the way one idea causes another is through the laws of the mind.

At the level of the conscious mind, the force of logic rules. Logic is not a physical force, but it still operates as a lawful power in the mind.

Ideas are also linked to one another by patterns of meaning. Through similarity of meaning, one idea attracts another. There is a type of gravity in the ideaosphere. It is not based on the weight of the matter but on the similarity of meaning ("like attracts like"). At the subconscious level of the mind, the gravity of affinity follows symbolic, rather than logical, patterns.

Although people may be separated by time and space, they can still be close to one another through the ideas they share. Ideas define the geography of a culture or a religion. A nation is a state of mind.

The communication of ideas may not require sending signals through physical space. Telepathy, for example, is an ability that goes beyond time and space. If ideas live in their own fourth dimension, then they don't have to travel in order to reach telepathically from one person to the next.

When an idea falls out of the ideaosphere and lands in one person's mind, it is very likely it will appear in the of another person, too. The same inventions often imultaneously in several laboratories. Einstein is said to have remarked that if he hadn't developed his theory of relativity, someone else would have, because the idea was "in the air." When an idea is in season, it blossoms everywhere.

A British biologist, Rupert Sheldrake, has developed a theory he calls "morphic resonance" to explain such simultaneous inventions. In his book *A New Science of Life*, he presents a vision of the transpersonal reality of mind quite similar to Cayce's perspective. His term for the fourth-dimensional status of ideas is the "morphogenic field." He suggests that mental events in individual brains are patterned by this fourth-dimensional field. When a new pattern, or idea, successfully resonates within the receptive field of one brain, it becomes increasingly easy for that idea to resonate within other brains. The more people that are able to conceive the idea, the easier it becomes for other people to have the idea. It is the way that the time for an idea actually comes. To prove his point, he staged a demonstration with the help of the BBC television system.

In Sheldrake's experiment, he sent field researchers to remote parts of the world and showed people two visual puzzles. They were both the type you have seen in the Sunday comics: "Find the figure hidden in this picture." His researchers measured the percent of the population that could detect these hidden figures. Sheldrake then showed one of these pictures on television, broadcast to millions of British viewers. Using a special close-up shot, he pointed out the location of the hidden figure. Sheldrake now sent his field researchers back out to these same remote locations, where the television show could not have been seen. Again the researchers presented the same two pictures to hundreds of people. This time, however, about twice as many people as before were able to locate the figure in the picture that had been shown on television. People were no better at finding the figure hidden in the other picture. Sheldrake suggested that, according to the terms of his theory, when the millions

of television viewers discovered the hidden figure on television, it made that perception easier for other people to see.

It's natural to think of your mind as something that floats
in your head. It's easy to imagine your ideas as little things
hanging around inside your brain. Try a different image.

Imagine your brain to be a television set. Imagine the
broadcast airwaves to be the mind itself. Ideas are vibrational
patterns in those waves. Airwaves permeate everything. The
airwaves don't sit inside the television set, and neither does
the mind sit in the brain. Instead, the brain is sensitive to
the energy of the airwaves and is able to tune in to them.

Cayce indicated that the individual brain resonates to the
vibrations of patterns that exist within the mind. The brain
tunes in to ideas that are in the air.

Remove all the television sets from the planet, and the
airwaves remain. The mind is a reality itself, independent of
physical bodies. The connection between the mind and the
body is the reverse of what we usually think.

Mind and Matter: Patterns of Oneness

A television set does not create the airwaves. The situation is the reverse. The airwaves drive the television set.
The pattern of vibrations in the airwaves determine the
pattern of activity on the television screen. Similarly, the
mind is the active force behind what we see around us.

The mind is a primary reality of its own. It is a universal
reality. It feeds us all with some very similar mental patterns. That same mind gives the world the patterns in
nature. As Herman Melville wrote in *Moby Dick*, "Oh
nature, and O soul of man! how far beyond all utterance are
your linked analogies! Not the smallest atom stirs or lives
on matter, but has its cunning duplicate in mind."

There is an intimate relationship between mind and nature, or between mind and matter. Cayce refers to this link as the "image." God created the world, mind, and nature from images. The same images that are found in the mind are found in the forms of nature. Another term he used was "pattern." Both terms are in use today to describe the link between mind and matter. Cayce would have us understand the mind and nature are as one—they share the same patterns.

Artificially stimulating the brain, for example, can create some strange visual patterns. Similar patterns will appear as a result of head injuries or taking LSD. These purely imaginary patterns, however, resemble patterns found in nature.

Recall Jung's discovery that the hallucinations of a patient mirrored the revelations in an ancient religious ceremony. Years after his discovery, the *Mariner 2* spacecraft made a related discovery. It revealed that there is a wind on the surface of the sun! Astrophysicists later discovered a comet wagging a tail of charged particles. They supposed that it was connected with the movements of the solar wind. A few years later, *Mariner 10* discovered that the planet Mercury also has a tail that always points away from the sun.

This story reveals a universal pattern at work. The pattern found its way into a religious ceremony and the hallucinations of a patient. It also expressed itself in the workings of the sun and its neighbors. As above, so below. Mind and nature have the same patterns.

Perhaps the most significant example of this relationship comes from mathematics, the queen of the sciences. Mathematicians give free rein to their imagination. They invent totally imaginary mathematical systems. Like science-fiction writers who make up fantastic worlds and then follow the implications to see where they might lead, mathematicians conduct research on their inventions.

Such is the life of the pure mathematician. Yet they get paid for it. They earn their money because their imaginary worlds usually pay off down the road by helping scientists.

Mathematical inventions often prove to match a newly discovered pattern in nature.

A recent example is the "fractal," invented by IBM mathematician Benoit Mandelbrot. We are familiar with the first, second, and third dimension. We have heard of a fourth dimension. What would the half dimension be? A fractional dimension is basically unimaginable except to a mathematician. Yet with this concept, Mandelbrot created a mathematics that made sense of aspects of nature never before understood. Fractal geometry is now useful for explaining the patterning of squiggly coastlines, of rolling hills and valleys, and of many other apparently random irregularities in nature. What began in the imagination of the mathematician became a tool for the scientist to explore and understand physical reality.

The Creation of the Conscious Mind

We can use images, analogies, and examples to point to the existence of the one mind as a reality of its own. Yet we still experience mind, and our identity, through our conscious mind. The conscious mind is the mind of separation. It separates our consciousness from an awareness of the one mind. Knowing that there is but one mind, what are we to make of the conscious mind?

Imagine that once, long ago, there was only the one mind. There was only being-in-existence, but no one to behold it. Then the conscious mind appeared in humans. People instantaneously appeared to themselves.

It was like waking up from a sleepy daydream. All of a sudden, people realized they were persons walking in a world. "Here we are," they said to themselves at the moment of their birth into self-consciousness, "alive in a world." Immediately, there was the question, "Where did

we come from? Where were we before now? How did we
get here?''

Ancient myths of creation, from all over the world, tell
similar stories of this event. All involve an act of separation. In the Bible, for example, God separates the light from
the darkness, the waters from Heaven, and the dry land
from the waters. Before this act of creation through separation, all was a dark, formless void.

An act of separation was required to create conscious life.
Why was this so? Acting as free agents in the sensory world
of physical reality requires being able to perceive ourselves
as separate from that world.

If you have had a child, or have watched a child grow from
infancy, think about the difference between before and after the
"terrible twos." That is the point where the kid learns how to
say "No!" and perfects it to a perplexing art. Prior to learning
how to say "No!" the child is simply a reflexive part of the
family environment. Not that the child is always agreeable, for
it may fuss, resist, and go its own way. Yet compared to
standing right in front of you, looking you right in the eye, and
saying "No!" the earlier resistances seem minor.

When it learns to say "No," the child's days of innocent,
instinctive resistance to your wishes are over. The child now
seems to know what it is doing when it says "No." The
child is intentionally opposing your will with its own will.
The child has become a separate being—and it knows it!
Becoming a separate being, learning to say "No," opposing
the parents' wishes, and becoming self-conscious are all part
of an important stage in the growing-up process. Without
this development, the child could never become a real
person, nor have a life of its own.

The act of saying "No" is both a negation and an
affirmation. With the power of the sword to cut and divide
in two, saying "No" both states "You are not me!" and
affirms "I am me!"

The child's development of the self-consciousness of a separate being is much the same as the development of the conscious mind in the origin of human beings.

The conscious mind is capable of focusing on something in particular by ignoring what surrounds it. When we focus our attention, we are performing an act of separation, saying "Yes" to what we want to attend to and "No" to everything else. If you didn't have the power to focus your attention, you couldn't read this book very well. How this book smells could capture your attention as easily as the words printed on the pages. The conscious mind is the mind of sense discrimination.

What distinguishes the conscious mind from the unconscious, as we learned in the last chapter, is this power of attention. While you are able to focus your conscious mind, your unconscious is picking up all sorts of other messages. If you were conscious of what the unconscious was sensing, you would be helplessly distracted. There needs to be a separation between the conscious and the unconscious mind, or else there would be no conscious mind as we know it.

The young child needs to be able to forget that he or she is contained within a parental world and be free to play and become involved in make-believe games to develop skills. At the same time, there is a need to also recognize one's roots and source of sustenance. There is a reason for separation, yet the separation is only in the mind, it is not real.

The ancient wisdom of the East recognized this important aspect of the conscious mind. It is expressed in their image of the relationship of yin and yang, shown in Figure 3.

The yin-yang symbol shows two objects. Can you see them? One is a black comet swirling around a white sky. The other is a white comet swirling in a black sky. That's right, there are two comets, but you tend to see only one at a time. Depending on how you look at the picture deter-

mines which color you see as the object and which you see
as the background.

Figure 3

Yin and Yang

Looking at a pattern and making some part of it object
and the rest background is the conscious mind at work.
That's the way it wants to see. It's hard to see both at the
same time. Yet the purpose of the yin-yang symbol is to
remind us that the seen and the unseen are part of the same
reality. It shows us the power of the conscious mind as well
as what it forgets in order to exist.

Yet that same power to focus our attention and to perceive
separateness has also made us appear to ourselves as separate from each other, from our environment, separate from
earth, separate from creation, separate from God. It has cut

us off from our spiritual heritage, the invisible bond that unites all life. To our conscious, sensation-based mind, there is no invisible unity to life. There are just a bunch of things, including atoms, rocks, plants, animals, people, buildings, and automobiles, that somehow interact with one another.

All religious traditions, in the East and in the West, have developed forms of discipline for the conscious mind to help it to wake up from its illusion of separateness and recognize its roots in nonseparated wholeness. It takes the conscious mind a great deal of effort to realize that the perception of separateness is but a useful tool, not the ultimate reality.

If we are to ask the conscious mind to surrender its grip on its own cutting edge of sensory consciousness, it will help to offer it something in return. We can introduce it to the *soul* of the mind.

4

The Soul of the Mind

*An entity body-mind was first a soul before it
entered into material consciousness.*

Edgar Cayce 4083-1

We've dug down into the depths of the mind, exploring
some of the fascinating splendors of the unconscious regions. At first, it seemed that we were digging down into a
dark cave. Then, upon digging deeper, this dark region of
the underworld of the mind opened up onto a vast vista.

Looking deep within ourselves, deeper than the subconscious mind, we see the enormous sky of the superconscious.
The infinite world within and the heavens above are as one.
What are we to make of this surprise? How can it be that we
have such a connection with the infinite?

The psychiatrist Carl Jung found that deep within each
individual, at the central core of their being, was a religious
entity. He called it their real Self, or soul. It was from this
level of consciousness that Edgar Cayce gave his psychic readings. He called the soul's awareness the superconscious mind.

While Carl Jung was struggling through his research efforts in Switzerland to understand his discovery of the universal level of the mind, Edgar Cayce was devoting his life in America to giving the universal mind a voice. Whereas Jung was finding indirect evidence of the super-conscious soul and examining its footprints, Cayce allowed the superconscious to speak directly. By going into his trance state, Cayce was like an ambassador of good will, helping the superconscious mind to speak to us and tell us about itself.

From this source, we learn something important about the nature of the human being: We are spiritual beings, we are souls. Our physical existence is a reflection and a by-product of our spirituality, manifested into physical reality through the creative power of the mind.

The Creation of Souls

As a child did you ever wonder about the origin of things and your place in the universe? I can remember looking up at the sky and trying to count the stars. The enormity of the universe was overwhelming. What or where was the earth in all this? And what of little me?

From science class I knew my body was composed of millions of atoms. Were all the stars in the sky like atoms, too? If the stars were atoms, whose body did they make? Was that God? If so, then was I a particle in God's body? Where in that giant body was my atom—nearer God's nose or the toes? Could God feel me, I wondered, jumping up and down?

Compared to the universe, I felt so tiny. Yet my mind, something invisible but still something I could feel inside me, seemed large somehow. It could reach into the heavens. Although my body could be zillions and zillions of miles

away from one of God's eyes, my mind somehow felt close
to God's mind, as if our minds might almost touch.

I can remember discussing such ideas with my childhood
friends. Outdoor slumber parties under the starry sky were
favorite occasions for such speculations. For us kids, these
fantasies were very real. It was all so wonderous and
believable. We were natural mystics. Sometimes kids can
be wiser than grown-ups. The image of each of us being
an atom in God's body is exactly how Cayce, in his
superconscious state, described the origin and nature of
the soul.

Out of a black hole that hid the original, dark and lonely
mystery, God burst forth in a flash of creative impulse. Like
an only child who creates imaginary playmates, so God
burst out into souls. The creation of souls was an act of
God's creative generosity. It was also an expression of a
desire for companionship.

How would you imagine it? How would you envision a
soul as being a piece of God? My childhood friends and I
imagined it pretty much as in Cayce's description, "an atom
in the body of God." Just as the shape of atoms resembles
the shape of solar systems, as an atom of God, we may in
some sense resemble God. As the Bible puts it, we are
created in the image of God. What does that suggest to you?
One meaning is that we were created through God's imagination. It's an important concept that will become more
meaningful to you as we go along. Another meaning is that
we are somehow a reflection of God, that we correspond to
God in some way.

Cayce indicates that the Bible is giving a true and accurate description of the relationship of the individual soul to
that of God. The soul is both a piece of God, right out of
God's mind, and at the same time an image of God. Cayce
used words such as "model" and "replica" when describing how the soul is a carbon copy, in a smaller version, of

the creator. In modern terms, we might say our souls are clones of God.

In simple terms, we are children of God. If God had kids, wouldn't they be Godlike themselves? But God's kids are souls, not people as we normally experience them. We've become hardened by our concrete, physical existence, and forget that we are souls. So to say that we are children of God seems only like a wistful, poetic image, certainly not a literal truth. It is true, however, and it is coming time to get back to that truth. It will set us free. It should also enhance our self-esteem and give us the will toward assuming a creative responsibility toward life.

In Shirley MacLaine's TV miniseries *Out On a Limb*, her guide asks her to try saying, "I am God." She hesitates, understandably, then tries saying it. I can imagine that to most viewers, watching Shirley declare herself to be God seems insane, at the least sacrilegious. In fact, many people locked away in mental institutions declare the very same thing.

Cayce would have us understand, however, that what Shirley is saying is essentially true, *provided*, and it is a big proviso, that we know who we mean when we say "I." It is not the ordinary "I" who is God. It is not the little self, the ego Cayce called the "personality." Rather, it is the larger self, the soul, who can claim some identity with God.

To most people's ears, to hear "I am God" is an egotistical statement. Yet what Cayce wants us to focus on is the spiritual identity of a person, the fact that we are souls and as such, a part of God. Moreover, as souls, we have all of the attributes of God. Not that individual souls are all of God, but that each soul possesses the qualities of God. Each soul is God in miniature.

It is somewhat like the waves on the ocean. Each wave appears like a separate thing, yet each is a part of the ocean. And each wave is water, like the whole ocean, and contains the molecular components of the ocean. The soul is made up of the same stuff as God and has the same characteristics of God.

The most important quality of God is as the creator. Perhaps that is why "the Creator" is one of the most common names for God. And as souls, we have the same creative powers as God. Hearing this, our little "I," our ego would love to have such power, and drools at the prospect. Yet once we begin to appreciate the nature of this creative power, and how it derives from the soul, we realize that it is a responsibility as well as a glorious opportunity. It is the role the mind plays in this creative power that is the essential theme of this book.

Dimensions of Soul:
Spirit, Mind, and Will

How do you speak about the soul? The word has a long and mixed history. Usually, the soul is talked about as something that we "have": we are not to lose it, let it be destroyed or tarnished, but we are to have it saved. It's something we are to look after, as if it were a thing in our care. Where do you keep your soul? Do you know where your soul is tonight?

Edgar Cayce turns our ordinary reality on its head. He explains that, in fact, we *are* souls. It's not that we *have* them. In truth, souls have us, *souls are us!*

The soul has created the body it uses in the material world, the body we think of as us. The soul has the creative power of mind, originating in the heart of the superconscious and extending to the fingertips of the conscious mind—that small piece of mind we identify as being who we are. But our bodies and our conscious minds, as we normally think of ourselves, are but the tip of the nose of the soul. Our true being is on a much grander scale.

As lofty and mysterious as soul may seem, we do have some instinct for it. We talk about a "loss of soul" when we sense that something important is missing in life. It may be love that is missing. It may be sadness at the loss of the human element in the modern mechanical age. It may be the spark of spontaneity. Soul refers to something especially human.

When we say that something has killed a person's "spirit," we are referring to an important and vital element of life. When the spirit of an activity disappears, or the spirit with which we do something is gone, we feel sad. We miss the energy and spark that the spirit brings.

We each have a "mind of our own." A person who can no longer think for himself is no longer a full human being. Followers of dogmatic indoctrination, no longer with minds of their own, don't seem completely human, but appear more like robots or trained animals. We say that "a mind is a terrible thing to waste," recognizing its importance to living a full human life of self-respect and self-directedness. When we criticize an activity as mindless, or mind-deadening, we are recognizing that anything that kills the mind is dehumanizing.

Having our own free will is also something we recognize as essential to being human. When we meet someone who has lost his will, we are quite concerned that something important to life is missing. We find offensive leaders who steal the will of their followers. We disapprove of torture and brainwashing that is directed toward the breaking of the will. To be forced to do something against our will feels dehumanizing, and we naturally rebel against such pressure. The freedom of our will is something we cherish as particularly essential to a human being.

Spirit, mind, and will are the soul dimensions to human life. They are mourned when they are missing. Each of these has soul connotations for us. Soul as spirit, mind, and

will is something that makes humans people rather than
machines or animals, free rather than slaves.

These are the aspects of soul that Cayce identified. We
have always known these qualities were important. We just
didn't necessarily connect them with the soul. Cayce would
have us recognize and appreciate these three qualities as the
dimensions of soul

He was specific in his reference to the "dimensionality"
of the soul. He wanted us to understand how the finite,
conscious world of material life necessarily interprets the
infinite. The conscious mind of the senses lives in a three-
dimensional world. We have height, breadth, and width.
There are also the three dimensions of space, time, and
mass. From this three-dimensional viewpoint, the soul is
also understood in terms of three dimensions.

Spirit, mind, and will are each a basic dimension of soul,
each a distinct quality. When any dimension gets shrunk to a
minimum, we feel sad. There is a deadening in us, a
flattening of our lives, as if we lived in a two-dimensional
world, not really human. To be truly alive as human beings,
all three need to be present for us.

Spirit: The One Life Force

Spirit is the life force. It is energy, the one and only
energy in the universe. God is energy. When God created
souls, this same energy, or spirit, became a part of each
soul. Each soul consists of the same life force as God and
the rest of creation.

Science recognizes today four forms of energy: gravity,
electromagnetism, and the strong and the weak atomic forces.
Theorists believe, and are attempting to prove, that all four
forms of energy are variations on the same one basic energy.

Cayce taught that all energy is of the same source.

Atomic energy, solar energy, love, hatred, etc., are different aspects of the same one energy. The first law of creation is that everything proceeds from the same one source, the same energy. That is the spirit.

As physics defines it, energy is the ability to do work. Energy is the ability to apply force through a distance or over a period of time. There is power in energy, the ability to affect change, to do work, to make a difference. Energy is the dynamo, the spark, the life. Energy is vibration, it is pure excitement.

We never encounter pure vibration. We always encounter it patterned in a certain way. This same one energy can assume different forms, different guises, depending on the circumstances. If life is approached in one manner, atomic energy is experienced. Through a different set of circumstances, electrical energy can be realized. Humans experience energy in terms of stamina, motivation, drives, and feelings. These are but different faces of energy. What gives spirit, or energy, its face is the mind. The mind patterns energy.

Mind: The Pattern Generator

The spirit in which we do something is the quality of energy we put into it. The quality of the energy has to do with how it is patterned. It means the ideals or purposes we have in mind.

The spirit in which we do something is often more important than what we actually do, for it reflects our intentions. As William Blake said, "A truth that's told with bad intent / Beats all the lies you can invent."

Love is the ultimate spiritual force. We know that something done in the spirit of love is done in the best possible way. In the Gospel of John we read, "God is love." That is the ideal form of creative energy. It is energy patterned as a caring, empathic embrace of respect and good will.

It is the mind that patterns energy. There is only one energy, or spirit. When we speak of the spirit in which something is done, we are referring to the mental pattern that is shaping that one energy. How we experience energy is a reflection of how it is being patterned by the mind. The mind is the second attribute of the soul.

The Mind of God that created the whole universe was given to souls at the time of their creation. All the wonderful patterns in nature are the creations of that Mind. The mind of God gave shape to the spirit by means of those patterns. That same mind is active within each soul.

Mind organizes and creates patterns. A good mind is one that is particularly perceptive of patterns. A creative mind can see unusual patterns that others ignore. An alert mind is aware, awake and present in a situation, ready to recognize old patterns and create new ones.

By working with patterns, mind is the builder. It shapes energy into particular patterns and thus has an affect on how the energy is expressed.

The desire for a new job, a new house, or a new relationship is a source of energy. It is the mind that begins to create patterns that will satisfy that desire, that will give shape to an opportunity. In the imagination new patterns of working are conceived, blueprints for better living are constructed, scenarios of satisfying relationships are envisioned.

The mind operates at several levels. We are most familiar with the conscious mind. But now we know that behind the conscious mind there is the subconscious, and behind that, the superconscious mind. Each has its own realm of specialty.

The conscious mind is good at focused detail, discriminating the finer facts of one pattern from another.

The subconscious mind is less focused, but it is better at

perceiving subtle or broader patterns that the conscious mind misses. When we can't see the forest for the trees, it is because our conscious mind is totally in charge. Lay aside the conscious mind, as in sleep, and the subconscious will reveal patterns in our lives that we hadn't noticed. It was through a dream, if you recall, that the student recognized that O,T,T,F,F were numbers.

The superconscious mind is aware not only of the patterns in our lives, but of the patterns from all our lives and the patterns of their interrelationships. Its access to universal awareness gives it a perspective on the eternal patterns of truth and law that govern all aspects of existence.

Recall our example from the last chapter concerning the girl with asthma. It was the subconscious of the mother and child that recognized the pattern that linked the mother's attitude with the child's physical disturbance. It was the superconscious that recognized the relationship between that pattern in the family and centuries-old patterns of energy that people had once regarded religiously.

Will: The Chooser

The mind can create endless patterns to direct and shape energy. To the mind, one pattern is not necessarily better than another. The choice of pattern is not the job of the mind. It is the job of the will. We have choices to make about which mental patterns will shape the flow of energy in our lives. We have that choice because we have free will. It is the third dimension of the soul.

One of the most significant choices made by God when creating souls was to give each soul free will. God gave souls free will because of the purpose God had for souls. According to Cayce, it is God's intention that souls be companions to God, not slaves or robots. Although that is

God's intention, it is our free will to choose this companionship, to ignore it or reject it. It is important to God that we
do have the free will to make that choice.

Think about it for a moment. When you spend time with
a friend, isn't it important to you that the friend *wants* to be
with you? If you thought the person didn't really want to be with
you, but was doing it for other reasons, wouldn't that affect
your feelings? When you ask your friend, or spouse, "What
would you like to do?" and the answer is, "I don't know,
whatever you would like," don't you find that frustrating?

A woman may feel ill at ease when her male partner
seems always to act in a way that is designed to please her
but that reveals nothing about the man's own feelings.
Likewise, men are not attracted to women who seem to do
whatever is asked of them, for they get the feeling that such
women would act that way with any man. A man wants to
know that the woman is responding to *him*.

We want the acts of love we receive from our friends to
be the result of free choice. We want our friends to *choose*
to love us, not to feel obligated to do so.

In the same way, God wants each soul to be a conscious
companion by choice. It is God's intention that each of us
realize that we are souls, children of God, and assume our
rightful place as cooperative co-creators. In order to fulfill
that intention, God gave souls free will and permits its wide
use. The soul is free because it has the will to make choices.

With the mind, you can think of many different ways of
spending your time. Obviously, you can't do them all. Will
is the ability to make choices. It is the choosing function.

We can see our will at work in what captures our
attention. This is our unconscious will, not consciously
applied. To a great extent, we have lost our free will. When
we are not conscious of our beliefs, our perceptions, and
our values, we make our choices subconsciously, without
conscious deliberation. Habits free the conscious mind of

having to reinvent the wheel at every turn. Yet habits based on old choices can prove later to be dictators that steal our will.

To regain the freedom of our will, we must become consciously aware of what we have been subconsciously choosing. Then we can choose anew.

Cayce wants us to realize that there is no power in the world that can resist the power of our will. Astrology, drug addiction, karma, ironclad circumstances, bureaucracy, even the laws of nature—none of these is stronger than our will.

Even the laws of nature are not as strong as our will. In this startling statement, Cayce anticipated modern thinking about natural law. Truth itself is a growing thing, he said. He indicated that the laws of nature are but habits of the universe and subject to change through learning and will. It is something to ponder as you begin to discover the creative power of the mind.

Creation: Soul Projection

Suppose you are feeling fidgety. Your mind wanders from topic to topic, your arms and legs are restless. You are experiencing energy that wants to be expressed. But what shall you do? You think of various chores that need to be done, but you don't know if you feel like doing them. You think of that painting or knitting project that is unfinished, of some friends you have been wanting to visit, or of a book that you have been reading. None of these things does the trick, and you fuss about as your mind continues to flip through its files of ideas, memories, and other images of how you might express your energy.

Somewhere in that process you find yourself cleaning up the house or straightening out the garage. It may have been a conscious decision, or you may have only stumbled onto it. In either case, among the various possibilities your mind

considered, you chose that one. Your will selected one of
the patterns provided by the mind for the expression of your
energy. Now that fidgety energy has been transformed into a
physical reality: your house is clean, the garage is reorgan-
ized. And you feel different.

This example is something that is familiar to most all of
us. It also illustrates a very important secret about the
process of creation. What began as energy, and was experienced as a bodily feeling, evolved into a variety of mental
patterns, or images. Through an act of choice, the exercise
of either conscious or unconscious willing, a particular
mental pattern was used to channel the energy into a
specific activity. The result was a physical, concrete reality.
Energy was patterned by the mind to achieve a resulting
manifestation in the physical world.

The sequence, from pure energy, through a mental pattern, and into an observable manifestation, is the process of
creation. Cayce expresses this process as a formula: "The
spirit is the life, the mind the builder, and the physical is
the result." The formula works in all areas of life. It is true
for the condition of our own bodies, as well as the creation
of all life forms. It is also true for the experiences we have
in life, as well as the course of history. What we see around
us and what we experience in life began as energy that was
patterned in the mind.

Look around you, at your living conditions, your job,
your family and the other elements of your life. What you
are seeing is a bit of history. The circumstances of your life
are living relics of thoughts you chose to entertain in the
past. Some you recognize. The job you hold now, for
example, you may recognize to be the result of earlier
desires, fantasies, and hard work. Other aspects you may
not recognize. There are probably circumstances in your life
that do not please you, that you did not choose. These are
the circumstances that you will be able to address as you

become more fully aware of how the mind creates reality.

Life as we experience it is a projection of the soul. The word *projection* provides a useful way to imagine the process of creation. There is an analogy I find especially appealing that was developed by Herbert Puryear and Mark Thurston, two psychologists who are experienced students of the Cayce readings. It involves the workings of a film projection camera in a movie theater.

Within the camera is a powerful light bulb. It only does one thing—it shines a bright, white light. The light bulb represents the spirit, the one energy of all creation. The projector accepts the insertion of film, transparent sheets filled with colored patterns. Whereas the camera bulb remains a constant, the film can contain almost anything. It is the creative pattern-making ability of the mind that invents what will be on the film. The film represents the mind's mental pattern. The pattern on the film shapes the light coming from the bulb. As the light passes through colored portions of the film, the light appears colored, even though the bulb is itself emitting only white light. The patterns on the film blocks light here and lets it pass there, creating the impression of shapes. When this filtered light is projected upon a screen, images appear.

The screen makes it possible for the images to be seen. Cayce refers to this screen as the "skein of time and space." The three-dimensional world is like a screen, or device that allows mind-patterned spirit to be visible. Without the screen, the projected images would travel along the light beam out into infinity. The screen "captures" the projected image, allowing it to become visible. So it is with life in our material existence. The existence of the time/space continuum allows physicality to exist for our consciousness.

What we take to be our bodies, the flesh, blood and bones that feel so concretely real to us, are really projections of

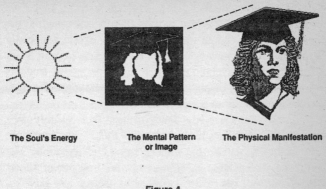

The Soul's Energy   The Mental Pattern   The Physical Manifestation
                              or Image

Figure 4

The Creation Formula

consciousness, like images on a screen. Originating in the
energy of the spirit, and patterned by our minds, our soul
creates a body in its own image, just as souls were created
in the image of God. Your soul "grew" your body from its
mind. Your body is the soul's physical symbol for itself.
Your soul also creates, by projection, the experiences that
you have in the movie you call life. The body that seems so
fixed and slow to change, as well as the circumstances of
your life, are as easy to change as it is to place a different
film in the projector. That makes the mind quite a magical
instrument.

The "magical lantern," as a movie projector was first
called, is magical indeed. You know what it's like to go to
the movies and get caught up in the picture. The movie is
hypnotic. We forget our own reality and enter the reality of
the movie. A light bulb is being filtered by a series of
colored patterns and projected onto a screen. Meanwhile,

we are transported to faraway places and taken on an emotional journey. We become part of another life, another reality.

The invention of the film projector has had a tremendous impact on our culture. No doubt its power is based on the fact that its mechanics and effects mimic something about the nature of reality. The source of the invention was also possibly the result of an unconscious knowing on the inventor's part of this secret of reality, that it is a projection of consciousness.

Life, like a movie, is a dream. We first imagine it, and then what we imagine we project. We are hypnotized by the projection, and the dream becomes real. That life is like a dream is part of the magic. That it becomes our reality is, however, somewhat of a problem.

Souls at Play Lose Their Way Home

Little Johnny was hard at play when it happened. Armed with his two six-shooters, one in each hand, he was courageously holding off a band of outlaws. He had mortally wounded all but two of the bad men and was about to face off his last opponents. He stepped out of his hiding spot and was marching toward his destiny, issuing the final challenge to surrender or else, when the scene was shattered by a piercing voice announcing, "John-ny! Come ho-ome! Dinnertime!" In an instant, the world of this little hero, who was about to be crowned and badged as the Shining Sheriff, shrunk to that of a little boy called home by his mother. As much as he liked to eat, he wished he could have taken his chow back at the saloon, where he could have enjoyed his reward with his admiring fans. What a letdown!

Johnny's situation is like Cayce's story of souls, except

that, unlike Johnny, few souls have heard the call to come home. The movies that souls have projected, their dreams, have become so real that they have forgotten that their creations are but playthings. They have forgotten about home. All they have, it seems, are their dreams.

Using the spiritual energy granted from God, and with the patterns in their minds, souls co-created with God the three-dimensional world we call earth life. It began as a legitimate foray into what a sensory existence would feel like. It was a creative extension of the Kingdom of God. But the sensory world, like the movie on the screen, had a hypnotic power. Souls began to get caught up in the world of the senses.

Souls fell in consciousness from their natural, superconscious birthright, to identifying solely with the conscious mind and its life of sensations. Like the two-year-old, souls had to say "No!" to their connection with the creator, perhaps to fully explore the implications of using their own will.

Relying on their own will, choosing the sensory world of the conscious mind, souls have pursued the hypnotic dream of their projections. In their enchantment, seeing nature not as part of their very being but as a playground for exploitation, they have enmeshed themselves in a mechanical nightmare. It is somewhat like the situation of the "Sorcerer's Apprentice" as seen in Walt Disney's *Fantasia*. Things have gotten out of hand.

What will be the outcome? There needs to be an awakening from the nightmare. This awakening is occurring. It is part of what has been called the "New Age."

Science, as a refinement of the conscious mind, not only has created some of the technological threats to our existence, but has also begun to realize the interconnectedness of life as well as its nonmaterial essence. A different perspective on life is gaining acceptance.

Yet the awakening is also part of an ageless process. God

has never ceased calling us home. There have always been those individuals who have responded to the call and have awakened from their sleep. They, in turn, have tried to help God wake up others. The pressures of modern existence have been a recent incentive to hearken to the call of the spirit.

Edgar Cayce predicted these troubling times, and advised that we view the pressures in our lives as an opportunity to develop a new mind-set.

There are those who believe that nothing that mankind can do will make a difference in the outcome of the world, for it is totally up to God. And there are those who believe that it is totally up to human beings to try to fix up what is wrong with the world.

Cayce's view agrees with both sides of this debate. It is the God part of mankind that is the ultimate power, yet God acts through the mind and actions of human beings. When human beings become aware of the spiritual basis of the mind, they become even more creative in their ability to help themselves, each other, and God to help make life on earth as it is in Heaven.

The Creative Use of the Mind

The bursting of Johnny's bubble, from the imagined invulnerable, conquering hero to the reality of being a little boy son of a mother calling him home, is something like the disappointment of the conscious mind in discovering the truth of its status in the scheme of things. As Johnny marches home, he feels that his he-man world has been forever stolen from him, that he will never get to play again.

Of course, that is not true. As his mother would be the first to admit, Johnny's play is vitally important to his maturation. While chasing the outlaws, he develops initiative, courage, persistence, and other skills and self-confidence that will help him in the world. At the same time, he does have a family life, and needs to eat.

Likewise, the conscious mind, when it learns that its reality is of its own construction and is contained within a larger, unconscious reality, is afraid it won't be allowed to play its games anymore. On the contrary, the creative games the conscious mind plays are very important. It needs to learn to play them well. Yet it does need to realize it has a home, one not of its own making, but one that supports and feeds it. Then it can be free to do its job, which is to play its games in the most creative of ways.

The mind is the creator of consciousness. With our consciousness, we become aware of aspects of existence that might otherwise go unnoticed. Consciousness helps the world come alive. What would happen to the world if no one was aware of its threatened existence? Becoming consciously aware of more and more details of existence, as in science for example, helps more and more of the world become alive and real for us. This creative part of consciousness seems to also be important to God.

In one of his prayers, Cayce affirmed that to God "we [are] as lights in thee." As a soul, each of us is one of God's ways of experiencing the world. We each shine our light onto the world in our own way. We each reveal the world to God in our particular way. Carl Jung, in his later life, imagined God as a giant being who was peering out from the minds of individual people relying on their consciousness to get new glimpses of the world. God's creation continues through our own, individual responses to life.

The way we see the world affects the way we respond to it. The way we respond to it affects the world itself. God wants us to become more conscious and aware of this fact so that we can assume more responsibility in our role as co-creators with God. We are given the freedom and responsibility to create our lives as we choose.

You can have it your way. What way will you choose? If you get the big picture, if you realize that life is a dream, then how do you choose what kind of dream you want for your life? The implications of such a question must now be examined.

PART II

What Do You Have in Mind? Have It Your Way: Creating An Ideal Life

Thousands of people suffering from physical disease, financial misfortune, problems at home or at work, and every other human predicament imaginable wrote to Edgar Cayce for a psychic reading. In the diagnosis of the problem, Cayce often revealed the existence of some unsuspected hidden factor. It might have been a condition in the body, a past life memory, the activity of a disincarnate spirit, or the negative thoughts of someone in the person's environment. Regardless of what surprising revelation Cayce offered, he also repeated what was a constant theme throughout his career of helping people overcome the obstacles in their lives. He insisted that the people drop the notion that they were a victim of their circumstances. In gentle ways, in ways that were forceful and direct, or in an indirect manner, Cayce indicated that we are the creators of our own troublesome circumstances. If we will assume the responsibility for our misfortunes, we can then create our own fortunes.

Cayce did not share this revelation to blame us for our problems, to accuse us, or to make us feel bad. He was offering a gift, a road to freedom and to the inheritance of our divine birthright as creative souls.

His message was actually a restatement of the ancient and timeless revelation of all mystical experience. The "Perennial Philosophy," the universal core of all religions, states, "That art thou!" You, God, and reality are one. What you meet in life, as Cayce would say, is your self, the reflection of a soul projecting into the three-dimensional world. Cayce explained in great detail the meaning of this perennial wisdom. His explanation ranged from the most general of religious truths to the most specific facts of psychological functioning and the workings of the body.

Today this precept has become the motto of the New Age: "You are a God! You create your own reality." *The Course in Miracles*, EST training, Shirley MacLaine's workshops, and many others are based on this precept. Recognizing the power of the mind to shape our lives is indeed an important part of the new way of thinking that characterizes the New Age. If you suspect that those slogans, however, are a bit inflated, then you have detected, in fact, their fatal flaw. To assume that you are a god and that you create your own reality gives you a burden that can be too heavy to carry. The value of the Cayce readings on this topic is that it presents the notion of creating your own reality in a manner that avoids the pitfall of increased self-aggrandizement and self-blame. In this section of the book, therefore, we will discover how Cayce approached the question of creating an ideal life.

First we will explore the proposition that there is no objective reality independent of a subjective point of view. Such an idea is the modern scientific and philosophical equivalent of the Perennial Philosophy. The principle of universal subjectivity forces you to decide upon what subjective viewpoint you wish to adopt.

At this crucial point, Cayce indicates the importance of

establishing your values, especially spiritual values. He considered the choice of a spiritual ideal the most important task we have in life. In the exploration of this topic, we will learn about the role of ideals in shaping reality. Here is where Cayce will help us avoid the pitfall usually encountered by the naive application of the slogan "You create your own reality."

We will then follow Cayce's prescription for using an ideal to deal with life circumstances and to mold them to match our values. The way ideals shape the creative powers of the mind is through our attitudes. Attitudes can be used creatively to reshape circumstances. How we respond to a situation, and whether the situation claims us as its victim or we claim it to be our opportunity for growth, is a matter of attitude.

Mind is the builder and the physical is the result. Attitudes become reflected in physical reality, in the health of our body and in the physical circumstances of our lives. Cayce also knew the secret of using a reverse strategy, and we will learn how to use the physical level of existence to gain leverage to change destructive attitudes and emotional states. Even when we feel caught in the trap of a negative mental framework, there is something we can do to free ourselves from its grip.

Finally, we will learn about the use of the will in creating an ideal life. Cayce appreciated the proper use of willpower but wanted us to learn how to take advantage of a higher level of will. The use of willpower can be a tiring exercise and is limited in its effectiveness. Ideals have a will of their own, and we can learn how to harness their power. Finding the harmonious marriage between conscious willpower and divine will transforms the challenge of creating one's own reality to the opportunity for spiritual self-realization.

You are not a passive target of the arrows of misfortune,

but the active creator of your life. Your life, and everything you experience in it, is a creation and a reflection of the ideas and values you accept. You can choose to take this fact and blame yourself for your misfortunes, or you can use it to take charge and create an ideal life. Begin by trying to look at your problem as an opportunity to learn something about yourself and as an opportunity to develop new skills and new levels of awareness. By patient practice, you can develop the ability to master everything

5

Reality Is a
Subjective Experience

*That ye think, that ye put your mind to work
upon, to live upon, to feed upon, to live with, to
abide with, to associate with in the mind, that your
soul-body becomes! That is the law. That is the
destiny. That is as from the beginning, that each
thought of the Creator bore within itself its own
fruit as from the beginning.*

Edgar Cayce 262-78

Two people looking up at the clouds will see different
patterns in the sky. One may see a giant riding in a carriage
while the other sees a giraffe. We recognize in this situation
that what each person sees is something subjective, something based on the person's own needs and interests. On the
other hand, we realize that the cloud is actually a floating
mass of water vapor. That's what we call *objective* reality.

From an early age we learn the difference between subjective and objective. Subjective is what we feel, what we wish
for or fear. Subjective is our personal point of view. Objec-

tive is what is really there, the plain truth. Knowing the difference between objective reality and subjective belief is the basis of sound mental health.

This obvious truth is fundamental to our upbringing and to our worldview. To contradict it will cause objections, create confusions, and even elicit fears. Nevertheless, let it be said: there is no objective reality, only subjective experience.

We have examined Cayce's metaphysical model that explains the source of this subjectivity. Physical reality is the by-product of the mind's mental patterns giving form to the one single energy of creation.

Cayce also expressed this point of view in more practical terms. He often remarked that the thoughts a person entertains shape the experiences the person encounters. He was fond of quoting from Proverbs: "As he thinketh in his heart, so is he." (27:3) Were he alive today, he might well quote the Beatles: "What's within you is without you." Our life circumstances reflect the history of our thought patterns.

Our expectations, our beliefs, and even the thoughts we use to understand our world determine what we experience. We see what we understand. Perhaps that is why, in our language, "I see" and "I understand" mean essentially the same thing. Each person's experience is subjective, a personal point of view. There is no other reality.

We may regard science as the ultimate in human objectivity. It is a questionable assumption. Science is governed by the same expectancy principle, because science is an activity of human beings. When confronted by scientists wishing to test his ideas, Cayce questioned the purposes of the scientists. He knew that behind their instruments and their methodologies there was the same subjectivity as in any other area of human experience. This subjectivity expresses itself in expectations, in purposes and attitudes. Science creates a reality to match its vision.

The purpose of this chapter is to explore the assumption that there is such a thing as objectivity. We'll look at what we typically assume to be examples of objective processes. We'll see that there is good reason to suspect the presence of subjectivity in any experience of reality.

Expectations Create Reality: The "Rosenthal Effect"

We spend much of our lives interacting with people. People play a role in many of our endeavors. How we get along with others has a lot to do with our successes and failures. How do people respond to you? Do you find them to be kind and helpful, or do they stand in your way? Do they please you or annoy you?

The truth of the matter is that people will tend to mirror back to you your own expectations. The way they treat you reveals the thoughts you carry, your assumptions and beliefs. What you expect from people tends to become a self-fulfilling prophecy.

Consider the case of psychologists. They study people in the laboratory using scientific methods. They are highly trained in the careful observation of people's behaviors in strictly controlled situations. Psychologists have found, however, that their experiments also tend to create the very reality their research is supposed to objectively observe and measure. Self-fulfilling prophecies occur in laboratory research as well as in daily life.

This disturbing fact is sometimes called the "Rosenthal effect," named after the Harvard psychologist Robert Rosenthal, who first discovered it. I'm going to go into some detail, because it shows, in a way that is rarely considered, that our expectations are indeed self-fulfilling. It will make you think twice about how you interact with other people.

The experimental subjects in Rosenthal's original research weren't the usual ones. He studied research psychologists while they performed their own experiments. He would recruit ten researchers to each perform a certain experiment that he had designed. He would ask them. "Find out if it is really true that . . ." and then he would tell them his hypothesis. However, he didn't tell them all the same thing. He told half the researchers that his theory was one way, while he told the others that his idea was the reverse. Then he sent them to work in the laboratory and awaited their results. For the most part, the researchers returned with results that *confirmed what they thought to be the hypothesis*.

Rosenthal and others have confirmed this phenomenon in hundreds of experiments. Some have involved the researchers' testing human subjects on various tasks: studies of perception and learning, personality and intelligence testing, and studies of physical reactions within the body. Others have involved researchers working with animals. The results have all been the same. Somehow the researchers unintentionally affected the people or the animals they were studying to produce the results they were expecting.

You can imagine how upsetting the Rosenthal effect has been to the science of psychology. Many experiments have been conducted to find out the source of this problem. The first suspect was observational error. For hundreds of years we have known that scientists make mistakes, either in what they observe or how they record their observations. More often than not, the errors are in favor of the experimenter's bias. Errors of this sort, however, are rarely large enough to account for the Rosenthal effect. In fact, even when the experimenter is only conducting the experiment and not recording the data, Rosenthal's expectancy effect still occurs!

Then researchers began to observe experimenters through one-way mirrors, to see if they could find out if experimenters behaved in some manner that could explain their ability to produce the results that they were expecting. In this way it was discovered that it was indeed because experimenters interacted differently with their subjects in small, but apparently significant, ways that they led their subjects to confirm their expectations. How this happens is still not totally clear.

In one research project, for example, involving an experiment comparing "smart" with "dull" mice, the observer saw the experimenters handle more often the mice they believed to be smarter, giving them, literally, "more strokes." On the other hand, the experimenters talked more to the mice they believed to be duller. Is it possible that handling mice makes them do better at their tasks, while talking to them makes them do less well? When you try to think of an answer to this question, keep in mind that the Rosenthal effect has also occurred when experimenters were studying microscopic worms!

Because of the tremendous implications, researchers have conducted hundreds of experiments studying experimenters' interaction with human subjects. Examining movies and videotapes of an experimenter's behavior has revealed many disturbing facts. In another example, experimenters, both male and female, tended to smile more at female subjects than at male subjects. Many so-called "scientific facts" about the differences between the sexes may be the unintentional effect of sex stereotypes on the behavior of experimenters. This unfortunate effect occurs because experimental subjects behave differently when they receive a smile!

Smiles aren't the only thing that affect the experimental subject. The experimenter's sex and personality, need for power or approval, personal warmth, degree of anxiousness, and talkativeness affect the way a subject responds in an experiment. Whether the experimenter has had a good day or a bad day affects the outcome of the experiment. It has even been demonstrated that whether the experimenter is sweating or not, or how fast the experimenter is breathing, also affects the subject's behavior!

What isn't clear, but is now an active area of current research, is how the experimenter communicates his or her scientific expectations to the subjects through such acts as sweating or bodily movements. From what we've learned about subliminal perception, it shouldn't be a surprise that a subject would subconsciously notice such details about the experimenter's behavior. Perhaps the communication occurs through the subconscious—through that invisible link between minds.

Experiments attempting to control the Rosenthal effect have discovered how pervasive it can be. It seems almost impossible to prevent. It is able to seep through so many boundaries, however, that it almost does seem psychic.

Even when the experimenters conduct their experiments through remote control, the effect is evident. In one case, researchers had the experimenters give their instructions to the subjects on a tape recorder. There was no personal contact with the subjects. Nevertheless, the experimenter's expectancy was somehow relayed to the subjects and affected the results. In another case, experimenters used proxies to conduct the experiment. These assistants didn't know the experimenters' expectancies, yet they still affected the subjects in such a way to confirm those expectations.

If well-trained psychologists tend to confirm their expectations in their scientifically controlled experiments with people, you may suspect that it is quite likely that in your own interactions with people, you also tend to confirm your expectations. The Rosenthal effect shows us all that our expectations about how people are going to behave around us are indeed self-fulfilling.

Sensation Is Subjective

Social relations are certainly a subjective matter. So let's bring our examination of subjectivity down a notch to a more concrete level. Let's look at the senses, our eyes and our ears, and how they perceive the facts of reality. Aren't our senses themselves objective? Don't our eyes, ears, nose, tongue, fingers, and other physical organs of perception within our body tell us about the world of reality?

We don't experience the chemical interactions that occur on our tongue or in our nose. What we actually experience are tastes and smells. The chemical compounds that excite these events don't themselves contain the emotional reactions we experience. The joy in the smell of freshly baked bread is in the mind.

We don't experience the pulsing of physical energy in the air that vibrates in our ears. What we do experience is sound. Sound is a mental event, not a physical one. There is nothing in the physical characteristics of the pulsating air in the opera house that would explain why so many people are crying.

We don't directly experience the electromagnetic energy that hits our eyes; we experience light. Light is a subjective experience, a creation of the mind. We don't experience the wavelength of this energy; we experience color. Color isn't an aspect of the objective world, it is an attribute of the mind.

Our physical senses respond to physical processes in the external, objective world, but what we experience are subjective phenomena created by the mind. A cluster of photons passes through the eye's pupil and reach the retina. There they stimulate nerve endings on the surface of the retina. These nerves send electrochemical impulses to the brain. Then nerve cells within the brain fire. A chemical chain reaction occurs, moving from the surface of the retina to the inner part of the brain. We experience none of this. We experience the sensation of light.

Our senses don't speak objectively, but in a subjective language of their own. They don't inform us of the actual physical events that are stimulating them. Instead, they provide us with subjective sensations that are the stuff of the mind. Sensations are a subjective translation of physical events into psychological experiences.

Translating physical processes into mental events isn't the only subjectivity of sensation.

The Senses Are Biased

Another dimension of subjectivity exists because the relationship between the physical events that stimulate the senses and the sense impression that it creates isn't a simple one. Twice the light isn't always twice as bright. It depends upon the situation. A candle in the dark appears brighter than at midday. Plain rice is very tasty when you are very hungry. Red glows when placed against green, but is dull next to orange.

The mind uses the brain in complex ways to form its experiences. When forming a sense impression, it takes into account contrast, changes in levels of stimulation, movement, relative sizes, timing, and a host of other physical relationships among the available stimuli. The world of perceptual illusions is an entertaining place to discover how sensations fool the mind. Illusions have revealed to psychologists just how innocently and creatively the mind interprets its sensations.

The mind designs its perceptual system to optimize its functioning for the most common circumstances. In order to achieve this optimal performance, it sacrifices accuracy under certain conditions. For example, our senses pay attention primarily to changes in stimulation. There is no information in the status quo; only change is news.

Our nervous system expresses this bias for change by tiring of sensing the same old thing. Most nerve cells can't fire time after time in quick succession. It's called fatigue. Nerve networks will stop passing a message if it continues to be the same one. This process is called inhibition. You hear the air conditioner when it first comes on, but soon its sound fades away. It has been inhibited. When the air conditioner turns off again, the silence is very loud.

You can experience some intriguing effects of this aspect of your perceptual system by discovering the visual afterimage phenomenon. Look at a solid black square against a white background. Now take away the black square and look at the white background alone. You will see a white square glowing brighter on the paper. That is the afterimage. Staring at the black square has tired your eyes of the message. It begins to block the "black square" message from its neuronal firing. When you take away the black square and look at the white paper underneath, your brain interprets the retina's inhibition of "black square" information as meaning "white square." That area of the paper is so "un-black" that it appears whiter than white.

Afterimages appear in all the senses. There are afterimages of color. Try looking at a red square and the afterimage will be green. There are afterimages in bodily sensations. Taking off your roller skates after an afternoon's ride makes your feet feel so light you can almost fly. Tastes leave images. After eating a sweet roll, orange juice is too sour to drink.

Afterimages are one class of contrast effects. They are produced by your senses inhibiting the impression from a stimulus that remains constant, only to be caught overcompensating when a stimulus of opposite characteristics is presented.

Contrast effects are but one example of an unexpected consequence of what is, in most circumstances, a useful bias within the nervous system. It can lead to some powerful subjective experiences that go beyond simple perceptual illusions. A person who has suffered unkindness from others for many years will perceive someone who extends even the most basic consideration as a wondrous saint.

Science Is Subjective

Sensory information, the most mechanical foundation of our experience of the world, is highly subjective. It is a creative interpretation of physical data, data that is largely invisible to the conscious mind. We are utterly vulnerable to this level of basic subjectivity. Knowing about it doesn't help. Most perceptual illusions persist in spite of their being explained. This level of subjectivity is inherent in the way the mind designs the wiring of the brain.

While the senses aren't accurate and have built-in biases, we might expect that science, with it's high-powered measuring instruments, can perceive reality objectively. Whether or not we value science and technology, we all respect its power. We hold it up as representing the ideal of objectivity.

Our faith in the pure objectivity of science, however, is misplaced. All science is a subjective enterprise. It is an important point to consider. As we consider some of the ways that subjectivity affects science, we must conclude that all human experience must also be subjective. You may well come to the conclusion, as have several other philosophers, that objective reality, if it exists at all, remains unknown, and perhaps unknowable, to human beings.

Science Is a Value System

Science is really the statement of a value system. What it calls its "objective" stance toward reality—detachment, analysis, prediction and control—is actually a statement of values. It is a bias in favor of a certain attitude toward knowledge.

Suppose someone proposed to get to know you. What if that person said to you, "The best way of getting to know you is for me to remain aloof from you. I will break you up into pieces and analyze your parts. I want to examine all the little facts of your life with a computer. I am going to learn how to predict your every move. Furthermore, to prove that I have obtained this real power of knowledge of you, I will gain total control over you, and make you behave as I choose." Would you rush to reveal yourself to a person making such a proposal? You'd probably be amused or horrified.

Yet that is exactly the stance that science takes toward nature. It calls it "objective," and values detachment over intimacy, analysis over experience, prediction over involvement, and control over dialogue. Women have sometimes recognized this set of values in their male friends. In fact, some modern philosophers have proposed that the supposed objectivity of science is no more than a rationalization of masculine values.

In reaction to some of the negative consequences of this approach to science, some scientists have begun experimenting with an alternative approach, one that values respect for the integrity of nature. Perhaps we can learn as much valuable truth about nature by communing with it as we can by poking at it or tearing it apart.

Science Invents Stories About Reality

Science doesn't touch reality bare-handed, but through the gloves of its theories. It doesn't stare with the naked eye at nature, but views it through the glasses of concepts.

We usually assume that science deals only with facts. The facts of science, however, are really determined by concepts and theories. Gravity, magnetism, energy, electricity, atoms, and other such terms aren't actual facts. They are ideas. There is no such *thing* as electricity or gravity. They are shorthand terms for describing how certain aspects of the world behave. They are concepts developed to explain the sensations and experiences of scientists. These are the stories science invents about nature.

The sensations, or facts, that scientists seek are based on the theories they hold. Without a theory to make it meaningful in the first place, a fact isn't even noted. The history of science is full of new discoveries coming from facts that had always been ignored as irrelevant. Scientists are like other people: they see what they are looking for, and ignore everything else.

I'm sure you've had the experience of being with someone who professed to understand you but who was dealing with you on their own terms. No matter what you revealed about yourself, the person didn't really understand your point of view. Instead, the person assumed an air of understanding and analyzed everything you said in terms of their own pet theories and ideas. They would only notice those things about you that were relevant to the theory. Wasn't it infuriating? You wouldn't say the person was being objective. No, quite the contrary. The person, however, might profess profound objectivity, but they would be seeing only in terms of their own understanding.

We all use models and concepts to perceive and understand the world. Here's a demonstration that shows the difference between the raw facts and experience. It shows how automatically we use concepts to form our experiences.

The example concerns a visual demonstration that was developed by a psychologist, Fritze Heider. He designed an abstract, animated cartoon. It was a moving diagram involving a circle and a square. He used a mathematical formula to define the movement. Imagine this: The circle starts in one spot, and then begins to move in a particular direction at a certain speed for a certain period of time. At that point, the circle changes direction and speed, and later it changes again. Using a similar formula, he programmed the motion of the square. He changed the numerical values, however, for the square. It started at a different location than the circle. It began its first movement slightly after the circle began to move, and all the other changes in motion were slightly delayed relative to the circle. After developing this complicated program, he ran the cartoon and showed it to people.

When people saw the circle and the square move according to the formulas he designed, what do you think they thought they saw? You can bet they didn't say something like, "Oh, I see, you've created a pair of equations to define the motion of a circle and a square. The motions of the two are correlated. Very clever." No, of course not—no one said that. Instead, the invariable and immediate reaction was, "Oh, my goodness, the square is chasing the circle and the circle is trying to escape!"

The observers, being human, immediately used their imagination and perceived the events on the screen in terms of the concepts of running, chasing, and escaping. They created a meaning for what they saw and attributed purposes to the two "actors." Their reaction was natural. Their perception has a certain poetic truth to it. Yet it is a subjective creation.

Heider's purpose in creating this demonstration was to

show that human beings respond to what they experience by organizing that experience into meanings they can recognize, and into stories that make sense on the basis of their previous experience.

The language of science, and the way it organizes its perceptions, is the same. The only difference is that the stories scientists create are more abstract and use more complicated terms. Humans, whether scientists or not, experience the events in the world in terms of meaning, not raw facts. There is little choice, except to choose which concepts to use when forming our perceptions.

Suppose you see an automobile for the first time in your life. If you "saw" it as a sculpture, the facts you would look at would be its shapes and lines. If you saw it as a container, the facts you would look at would be the spaces inside. You might measure how much water the trunk held or how many books you could store in the passenger compartment. If you saw it as some type of calculator or computer, the facts you would look at would be the readings on the dials. You might push buttons and pull levers to see how these dials responded. If you saw it as a conveyer, you might see how much weight it could carry and how fast it would go when loaded. In any event, the facts you would observe would depend upon your conception of what the car is.

The problem of how to understand a car shows that objectivity isn't simply a matter of being accurate in your measurements. Seeing what is really there—being objective, in other words—requires that you know *what* to look at and how to organize in your mind what you see. Knowing what to look for assumes that you have in mind some concept, or model, that applies to what you are looking at.

If you have no idea what you are looking at, but want to learn about it, you will have to ask some questions, take some measurements, or poke at it in some manner. What you learn about something depends upon the kinds of questions you ask. To formulate these questions, you will have to try out some concepts. There is no way around it.

Meaning involves concepts. Yet concepts are concepts, not direct reality. Concepts impose a subjective point of view. In a real sense, perception is idolatrous. We worship the concepts that form our perceptions and mistake them for the real thing.

Scientists are no different from poets, who invent connections between experiences. The poet understands love and writes that the rosebud opens as an expression of love for the sun. The scientist understands photosynthesis and writes that the rose opens in response to the sunlight's action upon the plant cells.

Science only has it models, its symbols, its metaphors, and theories. Science is science fiction, it is the product of the imagination. Science lives in a dream world of its own making. Scientists would agree with this statement, but you may already be rushing to their defense by pointing out that science tests its theories to see where they are wrong. The assumption is that science is objective because it considers the implications of its dreams, and invents tests to detect errors in the models. Science pinches itself to see if it is dreaming. Scientists do take measurements of the world, but sometimes their yardsticks dent what they measure and alter the nature of the reality that is being observed.

Science Affects Reality

We would like to be able to assume that there is a reality independent of our own subjectivity. Science develops theories about this reality and tests their adequacy. Testing theories requires performing experiments and taking measurements. The idea is to find out what is happening.

We have seen, however, that in the science of psychology, the experimenter's expectations tended to make things happen on their own. We have seen that science generally, as well as our own senses, tend to have certain biases in the perception of reality. Our observations seem to mirror our assumptions. This problem just won't go away, and seems to get worse the closer we get to looking at the bottom line of physical reality, the atom.

The deeper science stuck its nose into the reality of the atom, the more the atom ran away from the scientist's intrusion. Atomic physicists found that their measurements disturbed what they were trying to measure. They discovered an enormous catch-22 about the task of observing reality: observing something changes it.

The principle of indeterminancy, as science calls it, states that it isn't possible to make an exact determination, or measurement, about the condition of something without simultaneously changing at least some aspect of its condition.

The principle is really no news to you. You already know how differently you act when someone is watching you. If you have ever been the subject of an interview, you know that the kind of information the interviewer gets from you depends on how the person approaches you. The interviewer has an effect on you, and that alters the kind of information you have to give. If you have ever wanted to watch animals in the wild, you know how frustrating it can be, for as soon as they see you, the animals change what they're doing or run away.

The observer affects the observed. This effect extends down to the most basic layer of reality. Atomic physics discovered that it is just not possible to look at an atom without the atom's feeling an impact of the scientist's observation. To see something, you have to shine light on it. The light bounces off the object and strikes the eyes. At the atomic level, in order for the measuring instrument to detect the presence of an atomic particle, it has to have some form of contact with that particle. That contact, however, affects the particle, changing its position or its direction of movement. Seeing affects the seen.

What is seen is also determined by the observer. What is an atom? We think of it as a thing. We call it a particle. Sometimes, however, it acts as if it's not a thing, but an event, an energy reaction in the form of a wave. Whether or not an atomic physicist finds a particle or a wave of energy when observing these minuscule aspects of reality depends upon the type of observation made. In the subatomic world, reality is quite sensitive. It has a way of shifting back and forth, from matter to energy, in a manner quite perplexing to the scientist who wants to get a firm handle on what is actually there. What is there seems to depend upon how the scientist wishes to grasp it.

Many of us consider that the foundation of reality, the very basic reality, is atomic. If that is reality, then physicists have discovered that you just can't observe reality without affecting it. Reality changes the moment it is seen. It is quite sensitive to the observer. Experiencing reality affects it. Some physicists believe that there can be no description of reality without also describing the observer of that reality. Consciousness itself must be part of the equation, because it is part of the process of creating reality.

The Science of Subjectivity

When we experience the world, we engage it in an interaction. Reality doesn't just stand still, but responds to our glance, moves to our touch and reflects our assumptions. The world tends to mirror our beliefs, understanding, and expectations, and this is true even for scientists looking at the world carefully through technological devices.

There is a subjectivity both in our sense organs as well as in the scientist's microscope. There is a self-fulfilling aspect to our interactions with other people, whether we are socializing, engaged in business, or observing subjects in a psychological experiment.

The science of subjectivity understands that we are only objective when we recognize that truth is an interactive event. Observer and observed together create what we have called objective reality.

Facts, circumstances, and the other ingredients that would constitute the atoms of our lives are subject to our own creative perceptions. The first step in learning to have life on our own terms, to "have it your way," is to realize that there is actually no other way. We cannot avoid our own role in creating the reality we experience.

6

Your Ideal Life

*The most important experience of this or any
individual entity is to first know what is the ideal—
spiritually. Who and what is thy pattern?*

Edgar Cayce 357-13

What would you do if you were lost in outer space?
Everywhere you look, above you, below, on all sides, all
you see is the enormity of space—full of stars. Which way
is up? Which way is home?

There is something equally disorienting about the idea
that all our experience is subjective. If all we experience is a
reflection of ourselves, then what do we have to hold on to?
If expectations are self-fulfilling, if reality is our own
creation, then are we not caught in a vicious circle of our
own selves? Doesn't the science of subjectivity abandon us
in a hall of mirrors?

Janet's Predicament

I remember a woman, Janet, who came to seek counseling
from me. She was depressed and felt lost. She felt her life
was a mess and she blamed herself.

She had a good job once and led a creative life, full
of excitement and self-expression. She had decided to go
to college and get an education that would advance her
career. Before she acted on that decision, she got married.
Her husband didn't like her working. She gave up her
job for him. They moved to another town, and while
he went to work, she stayed home and cared for their
child.

Janet was satisfied with this life for a while. Then her
husband developed a drinking problem. He lost his job. He
began to beat her, not just with his fists, but also verbally
with words of criticism and blame. Finally, he left her. What
he left behind was not only a broken marriage, but a pile of
debts, deep wounds, confusion, and guilt.

When Janet came to see me, she was staying with her
mother. She had no money, no job, not even a driver's
license. All she had was her child, bills, and lots of guilt.
Her depression was twofold. First, she had lost her life as
she knew it, and second, she blamed it all on herself.

She didn't know how she could ever recapture the
good life she had lived before her marriage. Her self-
confidence was lost, and she didn't think she could ever
get it back.

She was angry with herself for creating such a mess of
things. She echoed her husband's opinion that it was all her
fault. She felt guilty for driving him to drink. She felt as if
she must have deserved his beatings. She didn't blame him
for leaving her. She was guilty, but she didn't know where

she had gone wrong. That's why she had come to see me.

She expressed a passing acquaintance with the New Age slogan "You create your own reality." I watched her use it as another club to beat herself over the head. Her predicament proved to her that deep down, she was a mean, bad, and ugly person.

The Trap of Self-Blame

It's a normal reaction to blame ourselves when we suffer a loss. It's an unfortunate response, however, because the self-punishment adds to our misery and further depletes our resources for recovery. In Janet's case, and I have seen too many like hers, the suffering was even further intensified by her elevating self-blame to a spiritual principle. If we create our own reality, she reasoned with me, then she created this mess herself, on purpose! Her reaction is an example of what I meant when I said that the idea of creating one's own reality can trap a person in the vicious circle of oneself.

How can you avoid that trap, or get out of it if you happen to get caught? The trap does seem almost unavoidable. If there is no reality beyond what we create ourselves, then how can we avoid blaming ourselves when things go wrong? If the world is a mirror of our own selves, then what else do we have but ourselves? There seems no other place to stand, no place to get a foothold to get out of the maze of mirrors.

Sometimes puzzles appear unsolvable only because we have limited our options by our assumptions. Consider this example:

Below are nine dots arranged in a square. Connect all nine dots with a series of four straight lines, but without lifting your pencil from the paper.

Did you figure it out? The task is impossible if you limit your options by the assumption that your lines must remain within the square suggested by the dots. The statement of the puzzle doesn't require you to limit yourself in that way. The arrangement of the dots, however, does subtly suggest the limitation to your imagination. If you can break out of that box, you can solve the puzzle.

[Note: The solution is to draw a horizontal line through the second and third dots in the first row, but to continue the line to where a fourth dot would be. From there, continue with a diagonal line that cuts through the third dot in the second row, the second dot in the third row, and down to where the first dot would be in a fourth row. From there, continue by drawing a line straight up through the first dot in each row. The fourth and final line section will then be obvious.]

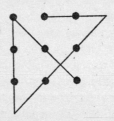

In the phrase "You create your own reality," there is also the suggestion of a box. Do you know what that box is? It is suggested by the word *you*. How did you interpret the word? Did you assume it meant your conscious self? Perhaps it could include your subconscious as well. Perhaps the metaphysical statement is actually addressed to your higher self, your soul. What if *you* meant God?

In an earlier part of the book, we examined Cayce's perspective on our spiritual identity. That entity is clearly a much larger reality than what we identify as our conscious personality. Creating your own reality is quite a large proposition, spiritual in scope. We have to interpret each word in the statement from a spiritual perspective. If we take the word *you* in its everyday sense and then try to work with the statement, we get into trouble. We fall into the trap of self-blame.

Let's approach the problem the way Edgar Cayce did and see if things don't work out better.

If You Are Lost, Where Do You Want to Go?

Janet's situation was not hopeless. It only seemed that way. There was another way of looking at it. I shared with her my impression that her unhappiness showed just how well she knew what her life was supposed to be like. "You wouldn't be unhappy," I told her, "unless you knew a better life was possible." I asked her, "What kind of a life is it that you know you're supposed to have?"

At first, Janet was somewhat puzzled that I saw her unhappiness as such a good sign. She was focused on her misery, while I was concentrating on the deeper feeling that her misery implied. She was depressed because she felt she had ruined her dream. I was happy for her because she knew she *had* a dream. I wasn't just trying to cheer her up, or get her to look at the bright side. I wanted her to focus on what was real and enduring rather than on what was a temporary condition. After all, her unhappiness was a reaction. It was really pointing to her dream of an ideal life.

Look at it this way. If all experience is subjective, if our experience of the world mirrors who we are, if we create our own reality, then what do you have? You can say, "All I have is me!" and look at that. You can also say, "All I have is choices," and look at them. If life is but a dream, then what dream will you have? The choice is up to you. Upon what foundation will you base your choices?

Begin by Knowing Your Ideals

For most of us, it is through having problems that we learn what we want to fight for. It is through becoming unhappy that we begin to question what we want out of life. Most of the people who sought advice from Cayce contacted him because of a problem. The problem initiated the person into a broader perspective on life.

When Cayce provided his commentaries on how the mind builds reality, he was not trying to tell people that their problems were illusory. When he indicated that what people meet in life is their own selves, he was not suggesting that they were to blame for their problems. He was trying to remind people that circumstances in life don't just happen, they are created, and for a purpose. He was not suggesting that people feel bad, but that they remember their purpose.

We create circumstances, from a deep level within our being, in order to learn from them. What we're all trying to learn is what works for us and what doesn't. We're learning what choices are good for us. We're testing our ideals and learning how to implement them.

Cayce would ask the person to consider what ideal was being tested.

Problems initiate us on the path of conscious spiritual development. Learning that our life experiences reflect who we are informs us that there is a path. The first step on that path is to become aware of the ideal that is governing our journey. The ideal is the guiding star that we use for navigation.

We begin with an ideal. That is the first, most important step, in our conscious use of the mind.

How to Choose an Ideal

What would make Janet happy, I asked. She wanted to get a job and she wanted the best for her daughter. She also wanted to have a man to love and who would love her. I asked her to reflect upon happy times and to see if there were other things that she wanted. She thought she had some talent, especially with people, and she enjoyed being able to help people. She wanted to develop that talent. She wanted to be good at something and to get pleasure from doing it.

She had mentioned things having to do with family and with career. What was it about those things that would make her happy? Why would it make her happy for her daughter to have the best in life? Why would it make her happy to be able to express her talent in a skillful way? I asked her to think about it. What did she sense in those things that made her believe they would make her happy? She said that it was something good, but she wasn't sure exactly what it was.

I asked her to close her eyes and focus on what it felt like. I suggested that she imagine the feeling and savor it. Did any pictures come to mind? Perhaps it reminded her of some incidents in her life when she felt that certain "something good."

"It's a rosy feeling," she said, "all around me. It seeps into me and I feel very warm inside."

"What else?" I asked her. "What else do you notice?" She was smiling to herself, then remarked, "It sounds silly, but there is a good feeling in my heart and it is pouring out of me. It's warm, pink and very clear. It's alive and it . . . it knows it!''

''It doesn't sound silly at all,'' I replied. ''What does this sensation of a good feeling pouring out of your heart remind you of?''

Janet was quiet for a while and then told me, ''I don't know what it means, but I am remembering a time when I was working as a sales clerk in a department store. There was a woman customer who couldn't find any bed sheets that she liked. She described to me the colors and patterns in her bedroom. I could see it in my mind and it reminded me of some sheets I had seen somewhere in our stock. I spent some time looking, but I found them. When I showed them to her, her eyes lit up. She was really pleased. I felt really good, almost glowing. I had been able to think of those sheets and then find them. The customer thanked me, saying that she appreciated my taking so much time for her, and especially for being able to imagine just the kind of sheets she would like. It seems like a silly memory, but that's what came to mind.''

I pointed out to her that earlier she had expressed a desire to develop the talent she had for helping other people. The incident that she remembered seemed like a good example of just that. We discussed the glowing feeling she had during that event. What did it say about why she was so happy at that moment?

We talked about how good it is to feel loved and appreciated. She described instances of feeling special, of being the only person just like her. She had felt grateful for that incident with the customer. Her love of fabrics, her knack for color and design, being able to help someone in a special way, being appreciated—all these things came together in that moment. She said, ''That's the way it's supposed to be for me!''

Janet realized that her experience contained two qualities that were important to her happiness. First there was love. She noted, "Of course, it's a good feeling to give or receive love, but more than that, it brings out the best in a person!" Her eyes lit up and she said, "There's more to me than love—I'm smart, too!" She described the second quality as something like knowledge, or intelligence. She called it "a knowing."

"If there's a God," she explained, "then God wouldn't just be love, like some people say, but a *knowing love*, a love that was *intelligent*! It's like, I want what's best for my daughter and just loving her is not enough—I have to really know her to love her as best as I can. It's the two together that makes the magic. By itself, love can just be a warm feeling, while knowing, by itself, can be critical, like an eye staring at you and seeing through you. What I'm talking about is like a heart and an eye combined . . . seeing with the heart, knowing with love. It's what I've been feeling in our counseling sessions. When I first came here I was knowing myself in only a critical way and that just doesn't work. It's intelligence and love combined that makes life work."

Janet was in the process of formulating her ideal. Janet's statement of her ideal was "intelligent love." Her image of it was a heart with an eye. That was Janet's personal statement of *her* ultimate value, her vision of the Absolute Good. Another person would come up with a different ideal. A person might formulate an ideal based upon a religious tradition, such as using the word *Christ*, or *Buddha*, to express the composite of qualities that came together in that religious figure. Another person might value an abstract expression, such as Truth, Beauty, Quality, Harmony, Oneness, Bliss, Peace, Joy, Equality, or Freedom.

In each case, the word chosen only approximates the ideal it is trying to express. A symbol or an image is also useful as an alternative expression.

An ideal is something for the individual who formulates it. It is something the individual *does* believe in, not something an individual thinks everyone *should* believe in.

On the other hand, one way to see if the ideal you've chosen is really what you want is to ask yourself what kind of world it would be if everyone followed that ideal. Would it be a kind of world you would want to live in?

It is often difficult to express our feelings or intuitions about an ideal. We can recognize an example of it when we encounter it, as in an experience we had, but sometimes it can be difficult to define directly.

What Is an Ideal?

One definition of an ideal might be a person's highest value. Janet came up with an interesting definition when she used the phrase "If there were a God, then God would be . . ." and described a certain quality. It was her way of saying that an ideal is an ultimate value, a vision of an Absolute Good.

To explain the meaning of an ideal, Cayce often used the phrase "perfect standard." An ideal is a standard by which we measure the value of something. Since it is a perfect standard, we never encounter anything but approximations to it in real life. It is like a guiding star, something we can steer by and aim toward, but which is never reached.

Mathematics is the easiest place to understand the perfection of ideals, because there ideals can be precisely defined. Mathematics works with ideals that easily exist in theory but are not found in actuality. A circle is defined as a set of dots that are equally distant from a center. That definition gives the perfect expression of the ideal of a circle. The value of a circle is that it is perfectly round. In real life, however, there are no perfect circles, only approximations.

A straight line, a square, and a right angle are but a few ideals in mathematics that are defined quite precisely. They exist, but only as ideals. Although we use these concepts all the time as standards, in actuality we work only with approximations. We all know what a straight line is, but no one has ever seen one. No line is perfectly straight. Yet we use the ideal of a straight line as a standard all the time.

An ideal is a valued pattern of perfection that is used as a standard of excellence, quality, or spirituality. Ideals having to do with spiritual values cannot be defined exactly. An ideal is contained in the spirit of the law, not its letter. The "Spirit of '76" was the expression of an ideal for the founding of America. The Declaration of Independence and the Constitution were attempts to put that spirit into writing. These documents are imperfect attempts to define the ideals of a nation. America itself is an imperfect expression of its own ideal, yet the spirit of the ideal is there, alive and functioning as a guide.

Ideals and Ideas

Earlier we learned that ideas exist in a fourth dimension, what we called "idealand." Ideals are similar, in that they live in an eternal dimension of their own. Ideas and ideals both exist as patterns of energy in the mind. They both operate through the mind to give shape to physical things and to events in the world. Yet ideals and ideas are not the same.

There is an idea called a "mousetrap." The idea itself is in another dimension. You could destroy all the mousetraps in the world, but you would not destroy the idea of a mousetrap. Like an ideal, the experience of an idea does not depend upon there being any actual examples in the physical world.

Unlike an ideal, however, the idea of a mousetrap does have perfectly satisfactory manifestions in the world. A device that catches a mouse satisfies the idea of a mousetrap. The idea of a mousetrap does not imply a standard of perfection that can only be approximated but never reached. While an ideal cannot find fulfillment in any concrete example, an idea can.

One mousetrap can be better than another. It is possible to build a better mousetrap. If one mousetrap is better than another, it is not because it is a closer approximation to the idea of a mousetrap. Both mousetraps fulfill the definition, but one may have an additional feature. A mousetrap that doesn't snap on little children's fingers is better because it's safer.

Evaluating a mousetrap for its safety is evaluating it according to an *ideal,* not according to the *idea* of a mousetrap. We can think about an ideal mousetrap, but it means going beyond simply the mousetrap idea. It means thinking about some absolute standard of perfection, in terms of an ideal like safety, humaneness, or efficiency, that would be used to distinguish a better mousetrap from an ordinary one. Yet a mousetrap can still be a mousetrap without being even close to an ideal one.

Because an ideal can never be satisfied, it acts as a perpetual motivator. An idea can be a motivator, but since it can be satisfied, it doesn't motivate for long. A teenager may have an ideal of freedom and daydream endlessly about owning a car. A car is an idea, and it can be satisfied. One day, the teenager will have a car and he or she will be satisfied, temporarily. Soon, however, the person will discover that although a car provides a certain freedom, in the sense of independence of movement, it brings with it certain requirements and responsibilities. Owning a car is not a free ride, nor does it allow total freedom of movement.

The *ideal* of total freedom of movement, its source deep within the intuition of humanity, has motivated many *ideas*. There was the shoe, the horse, the car, the airplane, and the rocket ship. The car came from the idea of a horseless carriage. The idea of a plane came from watching birds. Each of these ideas has been since improved upon, motivated by various ideals. Yet the ideal of total freedom of movement continues to motivate us to search for new ideas for transportation. Today we may consider its ultimate expression to be travel by thought, as in astral travel, remote viewing, traveling clairvoyance, or out-of-body experiences. In future years, the fulfillment of those ideas will probably reveal that the ideal is somehow still over the horizon. Unlike being motivated by an idea, to be motivated by an ideal means that we are forever reaching beyond our grasp.

Ideas and Ideals Create a Life

Although ideals never find perfect fulfillment, they are like ideas in that both operate through the patterning power of the mind to govern the shape of the material world. Mind and nature are one because of the patterns they share. Earlier we learned how image patterns in the mind give rise to the forms we encounter in life. This process is true both for the connection between the infinite mind and nature as a whole and for the connection between images in an individual's mind and that person's life experiences.

A person's conceptions, expectations, and beliefs govern what is experienced—even for scientists! It is the patterns in a person's mind that create the person's reality. It will make a difference whether or not ideals, and not just ideas, are among those patterns. A life centered on ideals will continue to grow fruitfully. A life centered on ideas alone, however, will run dry, because ideas can easily be satisfied.

As Janet and I reviewed her life history, for example, we encountered many ideas that had captured her attention: getting good grades in school, getting a good job, finding a suitable husband, and owning a home. Most of these ideas were goals and were capable of being achieved. She had, in fact, persisted with these ideas and achieved them, although some of them were later lost.

We also encountered some ideals: doing her best in life and being a good mother. With regard to ideals, since successful fulfillment is not possible, sincere trying is what counts. She had tried to live up to these ideals. Her conscience was clear on that score.

Janet and I were able to view much of her life history as a reflection of the ideas and ideals to which she devoted her attention. I pointed out to her that it was those mental patterns that created her life, not the "mean, bad, and ugly Janet" she had been blaming. If she did not like the way her life was developing, we should examine more closely her ideas and ideals, and especially the relationship between them.

We started with what happened in her marriage, because she felt that it was while being married that she lost the self-confidence that she had earlier. In particular, she realized that she regretted obeying her husband's request that she quit her job. Doing so left her totally dependent upon him. Why did she go along with his request? We uncovered several reasons.

Janet's ideal of doing her best extended to pleasing her husband. Janet's idea of being a good wife meant obeying his wishes. Needless to say, her husband probably agreed with that definition.

On a more general level, we learned that one of the ways that Janet measured whether she was doing her best was by the reaction of other people. When people were pleased with her, she was happy and satisfied. If they were not pleased, then she tried harder.

She gave lip service to the notion that you can't always please everyone. In her secret emotions, however, she hoped she could always be pleasing. Janet harbored the idea that it is necessary to please people in order for them to love you. Like most of us, she wanted people to love her. Her idea of people loving her was that they would approve of her, care for her, and be sensitive to her needs. Most especially, if a person loved her, they would not abandon her and leave her alone. Since her husband left her, it must have meant that she had not tried hard enough to please him.

Most of us can readily identify with Janet's system of thought. It is somewhat like an economic philosophy of relationships: I'll rub your back and you'll rub mine. The relationship is based on a system of exchange. I try to please you and you try to love me. If you have trouble loving me, I try harder to please you.

It is a common approach to relationships, one that certainly does not distinguish Janet as a unique individual. If it doesn't work, it is not because Janet is a failure, but because the system of thought is faulty. Ideas have consequences. If you harbor an idea, you'll receive its consequences. Janet experienced the consequences of the thoughts she held about love. The disappointment Janet experienced wasn't the result of Janet's failure as a person, it was the result of the limitations inherent in the ideas she believed in.

Given enough time, most ideas reveal their limitations. Cayce warned us to make sure that we held genuine ideals, and did not try to guide our lives by ideas. Ideas are tools to use, but must be under the influence and direction of ideals. There were many ideas governing Janet's life, but very few of them, if any, were under the supervision of an ideal.

Wasn't Janet guiding her life by the ideal of trying her best? It was a question I had Janet examine herself. I asked her to compare that ideal with the one she had recently formulated concerning seeing with the heart, "intelligent love." After some thought, her first response was that the ideal of trying her best left out some important things, like what her best really meant.

Did her best mean being satisfied with what pleased others, or did it mean what is best for others and herself as well? She realized that she never used it to mean pleasing to the best that was inside herself. In fact, she often had to ignore her own sense of best in order to please others. From the standpoint of her newer ideal, she was somewhat angry that she hadn't loved herself enough to develop confidence in her own standards of excellence.

I suggested that her anger was perhaps misplaced. We all need love. If we believe the idea that we must please others in order to have them love us, wouldn't it be natural to try to please others? I explained that I saw her as being very conscientious in fulfilling her duty to that idea.

As we continued our discussion of her older ideal of doing her best, Janet confided that she now felt that it really wasn't much of an ideal, if it was an ideal at all. She realized that the feeling behind it—in other words, the spirit of it—wasn't an expression of any vision of an ultimate good. Instead, it was based on a feeling that she was not inherently lovable. It was a formula, or a strategy, for obtaining the love that might not otherwise come her way.

Janet's life experiences confirmed the ideas she held about herself. No matter how hard she tried, she was not able to please her husband sufficiently, and her husband left her. The ideas we hold, even the erroneous ones, do tend to be self-fulfilling. In Janet's case, unfortunately, she didn't have a true ideal to live by, one that could have guided her in her evaluation of the ideas she used in making her way through life.

In the earlier part of her life, before she got married, her idea about doing her best seemed quite adequate. In general, she was dealing with people who were basically loving toward her, or who were expecting no more than a day's work for a day's pay. The inherent flaw in trying to please others to win their love had not yet been revealed.

Janet's approach to life was severely tested, however, when she got married. There she became involved with someone who was extremely self-involved and insecure. Her husband took advantage of Janet's formula for having a relationship, took it to its limit, and exhausted it. Janet's lack of an ideal left her vulnerable to her husband's insatiable requests that she live up to his expectations and meet all his needs. Her own ideas were of no help to her. Instead, they acted as if in conspiracy with her husband. As might be expected from their implications, her ideas about love led to Janet's burnout. Her husband then abandoned her.

Janet was not happy to have her ideas confirmed. Even when they are good ones, however, how many of us are truly happy when our ideas come to pass? How many times has it happened that you wanted something, a certain car, a type of job, only to find that after you had it for a while, it wasn't as satisfying anymore?

Perhaps you have sometimes suspected that things appear in their best light only while we are wanting them. When we finally get them, we see their faults or we lose interest. Cayce described ideas as "dead," because when they materialize, they lose their power. By themselves, ideas are unsatisfactory guides to living. They are fickle motivators. Ideals, on the other hand, reach toward the infinite, toward the unreachable standard of absolute perfection. Ideals shape our lives in the same way ideas do, through patterning, except that ideals don't lose their power, their magic, or fascination as they bear their fruit. They carry us forward to ever more tasty fruits.

Ideas focus our lives on results, the realization of the ideas, the end of a journey. Ideals have us focus on the process, on the journey itself. Working toward a goal is often more pleasurable than its accomplishment. Focusing on the process of doing a job, on how we obtain a goal, on the quality of the journey through life, ensures satisfaction.

In a study of creative writing, for example, two groups of students wrote poetry, but under different conditions. One group was asked first to imagine how well people would like their work. They were asked to imagine applause and congratulations. The other group was asked to imagine the fun it is to play with words. Then the two groups were asked to compose poems. The students who focused on the joy of writing wrote poetry that impressed the judges far more than did the students who were focused on the rewards of their efforts. Enjoyment of the process produced better results than did the anticipation of success.

Ideas and ideals both create the reality of a life, but only ideals will create a life that is satisfying. The true measure of a person is the ideal the person steers by. Rather than saying "You create your own reality," it would be more accurate to say, "You choose the ideas and ideals that create your reality."

Developing an Ideal Life

Defining an ideal is the first step in an adventure into higher consciousness. It is the beginning of learning to work with the mysteries of the mind for a more creative and fulfilling life. Developing an ideal life begins with the definition of an ideal.

Defining an ideal is not a once-and-for-all proposition. If you decide upon an ideal today, you can still change to a different ideal later. You may very well change your ideal as time goes on. Don't let the notion that you will be stuck with the ideal you state today stop you from formulating one now. In fact, reevaluating and reformulating your ideal is a normal and natural part of the journey to an ideal life. The important thing is to start developing your awareness of an ideal.

To begin this journey, Cayce recommended that you write down your best guess concerning your ideal and start keeping a journal. He suggested that you make notes about daily experiences in various areas of your life. Some of these general areas might be yourself, your family, your job, and your community. These will be areas that you will observe for the next few months to see where they reflect your ideal and where you would like to see an improvement. This journal process is a way for you to make an honest evaluation of your life in terms of an ideal.

Each night, make some notes about your experiences in each of these areas. Include your thoughts, actions, events, as well as emotional reactions and inner experiences.

For example, you may have had thoughts such as trying to figure out a solution to a problem at work. You may have had some positive thoughts about a particular success and some negative thoughts about some paperwork you had to do. Among your actions, you may have observed that you worked hard on certain tasks, while you procrastinated on others. You may have experienced some frustrations as well as had some moments of satisfaction.

Cayce suggested that you *not* read over these daily journal notes for at least thirty days. Simply allow them to accumulate.

After a month or so, set aside some time to review the notes in your journal. Take a candid look at the quality of your experiences in each of the areas of your life.

What were the best moments? What were the worst? You will be able to pinpoint aspects of your life that most closely approximate what you would consider ideal. You will also be able to find aspects that are far from ideal.

You can analyze the positive aspects to find out what it is about them that you particularly like. Your best moments are celebrations and expressions of positive values. Look at those values. There you will find clues about something that you actually held as an ideal, at least at that moment. How does it compare with the ideal you formulated?

It's also important to analyze the negative aspects to find out what it is about them that you particularly dislike. Again, you will find clues about a standard of excellence that you used at that moment.

When you were frustrated, for example, what values were being frustrated? Recall that when Janet came to counseling, she was aware of being despondent and angry with herself.

But it took some reflection to realize that her frustration was a response to the loss of something she valued. When we get angry or frustrated, or become sad or anxious, it is usually in response to a sense of loss, or the threat of loss, of something we value. Look behind the surface of your negative moments to discover the values you are guarding. Compare these values with your statement of your ideal. Does you ideal express these values? Does your ideal need to be modified to include these values, or do your values need to be brought more into harmony with your ideal?

Cayce's approach to working with ideals is to apply them to concrete situations in life. He followed the sequence of creation we discussed in an earlier chapter: The spirit is the life, mind is the builder, and the physical is the result. Thus, for any given situation, Cayce suggested that you allow your spiritual ideal to suggest a corresponding mental attitude, and let that attitude suggest a specific action or approach.

The remaining chapters in this section will explain the details of this process. They will show you how ideals can be used to both chart the course of your ideal life and to arrive at your goal. You will then have built a solid foundation at the spiritual, mental and behavioral level upon which to learn how to use the powers of even deeper regions of the mind to bring your ideal life into reality.

7

A Matter of Attitude

*There is much more to be obtained from the right
mental attitude respecting circumstances of either
physical, mental or spiritual than by the use of
properties, things or conditions outside of self. . . .*
                                        Edgar Cayce 5211-1

Attitude can be a dirty word. So it seems when you are
being accused of having one. Like bad breath, an attitude
can be a condition you don't know you have until someone
informs you, "You've got an attitude problem."

Your attitude is something other people are more aware of
than you. If they mention it, you often don't know what
they're talking about. If someone says, "I don't like your
attitude," about all you can guess is that you're not being
the way they want you to be. If someone says, "You've got
a good attitude," you suppose it means you are doing what
they want.

An attitude can be a social thing. Generally, if you have a
good attitude, people will like you. If you have a bad

attitude, you'll get into trouble and have a tough life.

I don't think that any of us got too much of an education in school about attitude beyond learning that it could be good or bad. Education's approach to attitude traditionally has been that it is the key to socialization rather than the secret of self-realization. I don't remember a teacher ever explaining that we could choose a specific attitude, from a wide range of options, that expressed our values and use it as a tool to shape our lives. No one ever discussed how to go about selecting an attitude and cultivating it as a creative personal tool. It was just a dirty word.

Edgar Cayce, on the other hand, was quite emphatic and specific about the importance of attitude. Second to working with ideals, he considered the choice of attitude and its cultivation a crucial aspect of a person's learning to use the powers of the mind. For Cayce, choosing an attitude and learning to cultivate it was a specific strategy to focus the creativity of the mind. Until a person has learned, from personal experience, the practical power of mental attitudes, none of the other powers of the mind can be mastered.

An Attitude Is Creative

The ideas in the mind fashion the life energy to create our experiences. Ideas complete themselves in physical reality and our expectations become self-fulfilling. To create an ideal life, therefore, we have to first establish what our ideal pattern is to be. These are the fundamental Cayce teachings we have been learning so far.

The next step is to focus on those thought patterns that are consistent with our ideal. It is a matter of attitude. An attitude is creative. Attitudes pattern thoughts and determine the ideas we use to create our experience.

Is the glass half empty or half full? The optimistic attitude draws our attention to what remains in the glass, while the pessimistic attitude focuses on what is missing. In actual fact, the glass is both half empty and half full. Both ideas are correct.

Which idea will grip your mind is a function of attitude. Each attitude leads the mind and its perceptions in a different direction. The two resultant thoughts have different implications for action, for your reactions to the glass, and for your future reality.

In terms of practical experience, then, we have a choice. How do you want to look at the glass of water? This choice is what Cayce called deciding upon an attitude.

An attitude is a way of looking at something, a point of view, a perspective, an outlook, a frame of mind. An attitude is like a window in a house. A window can be small or large, placed high or low and facing attractive scenery or a dismal view. How we face something is an attitude. Our attitude shows in the expression on our face.

An attitude is an orientation. Our posture expresses our attitude toward the world. The style of our physical gestures toward what is in front of us communicates our attitude. It is a style of interaction.

When riding your bike around a corner, you adopt an attitude of leaning into the curve, going with the turn. If you adopted an upright attitude, you would fall off the bike.

When you approach an angry person with a bossy attitude, you receive the full brunt of the person's anger. If you approach with a humble attitude, you find the person calmer.

An attitude is creative because it structures reality through its influence on the patterns of our thoughts. Like the concepts we use in perceiving things, an attitude influences which ideas will govern what we notice and how we understand it. Like the scientist's theories used in research, our attitude shapes how we experiment with situations. How we approach a situation influences how the situation itself responds. Life mirrors our attitudes. An attitude becomes an active ingredient in the creation of reality.

The Attitude of Self-Reliance

Of all the attitudes Cayce discussed, the one he considered to be the most fundamental is the one Ralph Waldo Emerson called self-reliance. It is a frame of mind that assumes "I can make a difference." It is an active style of interacting with events.

When people received a psychic reading from Cayce, his first suggestion, no matter what the problem, was invariably to discard their attitude of helplessness. The success of the specific help and remedies he might give depended upon the person's letting go of the attitude of victimization by circumstances. Cayce emphasized the necessity of an attitude of self-reliance, or, in his terminology, the realization that everything comes from within oneself.

No matter what cards life deals us, a self-reliant attitude insists that how the cards are played will determine the game.

The attitude of self-reliance rejects being the passive pawn of outside forces. As Emerson put it, "No man can come near me but through my act." It also declares, "No matter how oppressive a situation, nothing can take away the fact that I can choose how I will respond."

Where we direct our attention expresses and defines our attitude. An attitude of victimization focuses on the pressure of circumstances: "My bills are so big I am hopelessly in debt." The fixed focus is hypnotic and the circumstance is compelling. The effect is numbing and depressing. A self-reliant attitude, however, focuses on the available choices:

"How shall I manage what money I have?" Attention meanders among the possibilities, and there is a sense of freedom in the opportunity to make choices. The effect is motivating and creative.

No matter what happens to you, there is always the choice of attitude in how to respond. Realize this fact and you have a creative edge of freedom in dealing with circumstances. Ignore this fact, Cayce warns, and you will never discover the true purpose of your life. Even if your only choice is to turn a situation of defeat into an opportunity to learn something, that attitude can make the difference between ultimate defeat and survival.

Survivors of Solitary Ordeals

Survivors of catastrophes, where one's choices can be extremely limited, have found that the exercise of at least some choice was crucial to survival. The loss of freedom, whether caused by the constraints of the environment or by the limitations of the body in sickness, can be a source of depression and loss of the will to survive.

Those survivors who have endured this state have found that by limiting their attention to just a few things or areas of awareness, they can gain a sense of freedom. Simply deciding how to tie one's shoes can be a place to start. If the shoes are lost, or taken away, the survivor still has toes to count, to name, to dedicate the day to. Nothing matters except to find some place, even if only in the imagination, to play the game of attention, to make choices in that game, and to remain in charge of the game. So long as there is choice, there is life.

Richard Logan, a psychologist at the University of Wisconsin, studied survivors of such solitary ordeals as capture and imprisonment, long solo voyages, or being lost on a trek, and examined how they turned their situation around to help them survive. He found that they learned that their own attitude, and nothing else, determined how their predicaments affected them. Some experienced moments of transcendence while absorbed in their activities, even while enduring great suffering. For example, they would have experiences of merging with the environment. In such moments, the ego is lost or forgotten and the person and the environment become one. Even though that environment would seem distasteful by normal standards, when merger occurred the distastefulness would disappear. It was an extreme example of the dictum "If you can't beat them, join them." Not being able to beat the environment, these survivors found a way to merge with it that helped them keep their spirits up.

A judgmental attitude confines a person to an awareness of how things are not OK and of how helpless the person feels. By the suspension of judgment, the person is instead able to become more centered in the moment, and is rewarded with experiences of peace, harmony, and flow. Thus Cayce advocated that we adopt an attitude of acceptance toward everything we experience. A judgmental attitude cuts us off from the flow of life; while an attitude of acceptance carries us to the next unfolding moment and to the possibility of change.

A Sense of Personal Control

Stanford University psychologist Albert Bandura uses the concept of "self-efficacy" to explain the vital sense of personal control people can claim over their experiences. The term is another way of expressing the attitude "I can make a difference." It is an attitudinal, not necessarily a factual, control. Yet it can be the single most active ingredient in determining the outcome of events.

Research has demonstrated that people who believe they can exert some control over a situation will make more of an effort, will persist longer, won't stop when confronted by obstacles, and are less stressed by negative events.

People with a sense of self-efficacy have been found to be less fearful, get sick less often, and recover from illness faster. People who feel that they have some control over events find those events much less stressful. A sense of personal control makes a big difference in how we experience things.

If a person has no sense of personal control, the person is a hostage to circumstance. Bandura had found, however, if he can teach a person to control even a minor aspect of the situation, self-confidence improves and the person will gradually become in control of more aspects of the situation.

Cayce often recommended that we not underestimate the value of taking one such small step at a time. Many a time he patiently explained to a person who seem buried under unsolvable problems to simply make a beginning somewhere, anywhere. A ball of string is rarely in such a knotted mess that there isn't some place to begin unraveling it. We can pull ourselves up by our bootstraps if we'll first bend over and reach for the straps. It's a start.

I've experienced this effect myself many times and watched it with others I've counseled. Problems can seem so overwhelming that anxiety and depression further deplete a person's ability to cope. A free-fall of doom and gloom can be very frightening and intensify feelings of helplessness to the point of panic. At such moments, the suggestion to relax seems ridiculous.

"How can I relax at a moment like this? Besides, relaxation won't take away the bills, the disease, the lawsuit, or any of the other problems that are killing me!"

It's hard to argue with that kind of logic. It's an attitude of hopelessness that makes any action short of a miracle seem pointless. It's also a self-defeating attitude, rejecting any possibility of recovery from the misfortune.

With some persistent instructions to relax, taking advantage of the growing fatigue, the person can begin to calm down. With further instructions, the person can totally relax the body and begin to imagine peaceful scenes. In this tranquil space, the person begins the process of recovery. The mind clears and energy returns. Self-confidence begins to grow. In most cases, a person emerges from a few minutes of relaxation by announcing some strategy for dealing with the problems at hand.

By discovering that they could relax in spite of their problems, these people found that there was at least one thing they could control. They were able to stop the free-fall into devastation. The relaxation, beyond its sedative qualities, brought another gift. It provided a foundation of personal control that these people could build upon.

Thus research has shown that having a person learn to relax helps the person cope with a crisis. People taught relaxation prior to surgery experience less postoperative pain and recover faster. The relaxation itself is not necessarily the active ingredient. The increased sense of personal control is what makes the difference.

Turning Stumbling locks Into Stepping-Stones

An attitude of self-reliance says, "I'm the bottom line in this experience." A situation may seem out of control. There may be no choices for actions. But the self-reliant individual will find, or even invent, some choice to make. Choosing to remain calm, if that is all that can be done, can be the first step. By choosing one's own mental response,

the whirlwind of chaos slows down. The person has found
something to hold on to to begin a process of becoming
responsible for how the experience unfolds.

One of Cayce's favorite expressions was that we learn how
"to turn stumbling blocks into stepping stones." Perhaps you
are familiar with the saying "If life gives you a lemon, make
lemonade." If something bad happens, turn it to your advantage. It's not talking about whitewashing or ov looking the
negative, but finding something useful in ever ing.

Cayce's expression was somewhat more explicit. It means
using the negative event as a means of making some
progress toward a personally defined goal. If nothing else,
you can learn something from a bad situation, something
that you can use to help you later.

Thomas Edison tried hundreds of ways to make a light
bulb before he was able to finally make it work. When
asked how he felt about all his failures, he denied that he
had any failures. He indicated that he had learned hundreds
of ways *not* to make a light bulb. He learned something
from each experiment.

Deciding to learn something from a situation was Cayce's
favorite strategy for coping with adversity. No situation can
be so bad that you can't examine it to see if you can learn
something from it.

Cayce is not suggesting that you ask yourself, "What
lesson am I learning?" in the sense of being punished.
Sometimes our parents said to us, "I'm going to teach you a
lesson" as they began to spank or otherwise punish us. ut
instead, ask yourself what you can learn simply for the
purpose of asking the question. It quickens your curiosity,
helps you search for novelty in the situation, and helps you
become absorbed and to go with the flow.

Simply by asking what you can learn from a bad situation, you have changed your attitude. You are no longer
focusing on being the victim. Instead, you are taking control

by choosing to make the situation your servant of your education. It will serve your needs to grow in self-awareness. It will serve your needs to assume creative mastery over events. It will serve your development as you strengthen your commitment to your ideals. The stumbling block becomes the stepping stone to furthering your evolution into greater consciousness.

Cayce reminds us that the purpose of life is not simply to go on living. Although we need to eat in order to live, we do not live to eat. We live to grow in awareness and understanding of the creative endowment we have within us. By accepting every situation as an opportunity for growth, we invite the discovery of our purpose for living.

Cultivating Attitudes Consistent With Ideals

Maintaining a positive attitude in adversity is the key to survival. As someone once said, "Any problem that doesn't kill me will make me stronger." Growing from adversity is one way to claim victory from disaster.

For some people, discovering this secret in the midst of their misfortunes is what initiates them upon the spiritual path. Adversity forces them to explore the magically creative role of attitude, and they discover the existence of higher levels of consciousness. Ask many people how they were introduced to spiritual concepts, those of Edgar Cayce or another tradition, and many will tell you that it was through adversity.

But why wait for problems to begin the spiritual journey? We can embark on that quest right now, by looking at our attitudes from the perspective of our ideal.

The road to higher consciousness is guided by a spiritual ideal. The choice of ideal is up to you. It is your vision of the Ultimate Good. It is the spirit in which you wish to live.

To do so, the attitude you bring to situations will have to gradually become consistent with your ideal.

Cayce described the use of a practical strategy to bring about the desired relationship between your ideal and the life of your mind. You can use your ideal to guide you in your choice of attitudes.

In the last chapter, we described the initial stages of the process of working with ideals suggested by Cayce. It began with keeping a journal, and examining your experiences in light of your ideals. You can quickly determine those areas in life that challenge your ideals. These are situations that threaten your sense of peace and security, evoke reactions you don't like, or arouse feelings that are not in keeping with the spirit of your ideal. These are circumstances that hamper your freedom, depress you, hold you back, or divert your energies away from where you would put them.

Pick one of these situations to work with. Remind yourself that even though you don't always get to choose what you have to face, you can choose how you face it. Sometimes, that's the only choice you have.

Even if you have no other choices, remind yourself that you can choose your attitude. By deciding to make that choice, you can assert your own creative input on the situation. You can also invite the spiritual energy of your ideal to help you.

Cayce suggests that you next take a moment to reflect upon your ideal. Recall how you went about choosing it. If you used a past experience where you felt at your best, then recall that past experience. Get yourself in the mood of the spirit of your ideal.

Suppose your ideal is joy. Perhaps you made this choice based upon a memory of a sunny day when you took delight in everything you experienced. Your image of joy is the radiance of the sun with its smiling face. These are the various elements of your spiritual ideal. Contemplate all these elements to create in yourself a joyous atmosphere. Recall that wonderful memory of the sunny day and begin to feel the way you felt that day. Imagine being the sun smiling upon the earth. Imagine being a bird enjoying flapping its wings in flight. Imagine the soil of the earth warming itself in the sun. Think about the truth of your intuition, that all of creation is actually joyful. Be joyful in your realization.

Once you are filled with the spirit of your ideal, when you are in that mood, then look upon that unfavorable situation. From the perspective of your ideal, how do you view that situation? How does it appear to you? Imagine how you would react to that situation when you are in the mood of the spirit of your ideal. Note the attitude that you naturally adopt as you interact with the situation. What is that attitude? Can you sense it? Give it a name, as best you can.

In such a way, you can determine what your ideal attitude would be toward that situation. It is the attitude that defines the mental pattern that is most consistent with your spiritual ideal. It is the attitude that will channel the spiritual energy of your ideal into your approach to the situation. If you can cultivate that attitude, you will have your ideal to help you reshape that situation through constructive action.

An Attitude in Action

Suppose you are facing a bad situation at work. Your boss asks you, for example, to perform an impossible task. Maybe it's to develop and maintain a set of statistics concerning productivity. You just don't have the necessary resources to keep these statistics and also get your job done. What are you to do?

This sort of thing happens a lot. If you attempt the impossible, you will be overstressed and there will be consequences. If you tell your boss you can't do the job, there will be consequences. Can your spiritual ideal help you?

Suppose your ideal is love. Meditate on the feeling of this ideal and then ask yourself, "If I were approaching this situation in the spirit of love, what attitude would I take toward it?"

The first thoughts that come to mind might be to love yourself, love your boss, and love your work. What would be a loving attitude toward these three? Loving yourself, you would respect your limitations, care about your health, and would also have faith in your abilities, including your abilities to grow to new levels of competence in the face of new challenges. Loving your boss, you would respect the boss's perceptions of what needed to be done, care about your boss's needs and aspirations, and have faith in your boss's good intentions. Loving your work, you would respect its requirements, care about the quality with which it was done. You would have faith that it is possible to find an optimal solution to such a work crunch. Three attitudinal words are implied: respect, caring, and faith or optimism.

These attitudes certainly stand in contrast to what might be typical reactions to this predicament. You could easily resent the boss's new assignment. Your attitude could be defensive. You could look for reasons why you couldn't do this new job. But as you did so, your feeling that the boss didn't care about you and your already heavy workload would make you feel more desperate, resentful, and trapped. You might think of ways to get even, but as you did so, you would fear more and more the boss's ability to retaliate. Your defensive and fearful attitude could easily send you into a spiral of anxiety and rage.

If for no other reason than to protect your own sanity and to have some hope for coping with the problem, you would be better off to choose the positive attitude than the negative. Approaching this difficult situation with respect, caring, and optimism will be more beneficial to your state of mind than approaching it with disdain, resentment, and pessimism. It might also lead to a better outcome at the office.

Attitudes suggest the actions. They shape not only the way we respond inside, but also how we behave outwardly toward circumstances. Optimistic, for example, that a solution could be achieved and respectful of your boss's needs, you might get to work on the assignment while you also make a list of the consequences of attempting the job with inadequate resources. Caring about your boss's aspirations and optimistic that he will want to do his best, you might anticipate some of the negative consequences to him of your pursuing the job as assigned. Optimistic about your own creative abilities, you might try to come up with a proposal for a solution to the dilemma that minimized the negative consequences of the work crunch and resource shortage.

Then you might approach your boss and first tell him that you had begun the assignment. You would then inform him of the negative consequences you had discovered that would follow from your working on the assignment in the way he had originally envisioned, including those that would have a negative effect upon the boss's aspirations. You might present a proposal for how to restructure the assignment in the context of the other work requirements in order to minimize the negative consequences. You would leave the final decision to the boss.

In this hypothetical but all too common situation, you would be approaching your boss in a loving spirit of support, not confrontation. You would not be resisting the boss, but rather looking out for the boss's best interests, while you respected your own needs. You would be willing to put in an extra effort, yet you are not defensive about having limitations. By accepting realistic limitations, you are protecting both yourself and your boss from disappointment and other negative consequences.

This approach, although expressive of your ideal, cannot be perfect. You cannot control your boss's reaction. You can only control your own response. Don't expect to manipulate the boss into doing what you see as right, but maintain an optimistic view of your boss.

The example I've given of using an ideal to develop an approach to a difficult situation may seem too "idealistic" and not "realistic." Admittedly, working with ideals will lead to idealistic approaches—that is the purpose of ideals. On the other hand, such approaches need not be unrealistic. An idealistic approach requires more patience and effort, but may also, in the long run, be more realistic.

The *Challenger* space shuttle disaster brought to the public's awareness the tragic consequences of knuckling under to pressure from one's boss without fully communicating the consequences of pursuing an unsafe course of action. I know, from years spent training workers in the use of communication skills, as a stress-reduction and work-innovation tool, that most people respond with a knee-jerk reaction to receiving impossible job assignments. The instinctive reaction is a defensive attitude. It can be dangerous to all concerned. The idealistic approach is worth the time it takes to make it work.

Reactions at work are more often governed by ideas, not ideals. Ideas such as "the other guy doesn't care about my needs" and "I've got to look good or I'll be fired" are common culprits, and they are intensified by stress. One of two stereotyped, black-or-white responses to impossible assignments are usually evident. Full of resentment, the worker attempts the job, while developing excuses and ulcers in anticipation of the negative effects of attempting the impossible. Alternatively, the worker speaks up to the boss, but in a confrontational manner, communicating nonverbally if not also verbally, a lack of interest in cooperating with the boss's perceived need to get the job done.

The reaction of the boss is equally stereotyped. It needn't be that way.

As the stresses of modern life intensify, as the demands upon available resources multiply, the need for innovation in approaching situations demands better communication and enhanced creative functioning among all concerned. Working with ideals, in the manner Cayce suggested, becomes a powerful way of guiding such an adventure into creating an alternative future.

Healing Negative Attitudes

When you begin keeping a journal, you will probably discover certain negative attitudes that you tend to adopt. Once you begin working with your current ideal to develop positive alternatives, you will no doubt find, to your dismay, that some of these negative attitudes are clearly your favorites. You might have a hard time giving them up.

Thousands of people asked Cayce for advice on problems. No matter what the nature of the problem, whether it was physical, financial, or marital, Cayce often pointed to the role of a negative attitude.

Attitudinal problems were so commonly addressed that there are three volumes of published Cayce readings on this topic, covering over 160 different attitudes, from animosity to zealousness. Some of the most common negative attitudes were self-doubt and fearfulness, judgment, fault-finding or condemnation, and hopelessness.

Cayce traced the mental source of negative attitudes to a common root—an erroneous self-image or faulty understanding of the true nature of the self. He often used the word *selfishness* to express this faulty self-image. He was not referring to being stingy, or to being self-preoccupied. Rather, he was referring to being attached or fixated on a narrow conception of self. By selfishness he meant being hypnotized by the little self, or the ego of the conscious mind.

It is like the situation portrayed in the common dream of being naked or scantily dressed in a public place. It is a situation of extreme self-consciousness. All eyes are upon you, and you are hypnotized by your self's existence. Most negative attitudes grow out of the preoccupation with that level of our being.

Consider the problem of self-doubt. Cayce described it as a "shadow of selfishness." It is the result of a misplaced focus on one's own ego. Given the focus on self, the question naturally arises, "Can I really do this or that? Will other people really approve?"

A person asked Cayce, for example, why he always assumed that he would not be able to "put over" to an audience what was really in his heart. Cayce's answer was that self-doubt was the culprit. Having stage fright, or being shy, are instructive examples of self-doubt, because the self-preoccupation is easy to see. Self-doubt arises from a focus on the self and can be overcome by a change of focus.

I have found from personal experience that Cayce's analysis is correct. When I am shy, or have stage fright, or difficulty communicating to an audience, in public speaking or in writing, it is invariably because I am focused on myself and my performance. There is always a performance anxiety in self-doubt. If I shift my focus away from myself, and pay more attention to the audience and to ideas that wish to be expressed, my doubt vanishes. I become more concerned with introducing the audience to the ideas. I am out of the picture. I become the servant to the ideas and the audience. No one notices the servant. The audience responds to the ideas, not to me.

In this situation, I have traded in the attitude of self-doubt for one of love of the ideas and caring about the audience. I have become a channel for the ideas. Not only have I lost the unpleasant burden of self-doubt, but I have also experienced the pleasure of being able to ride the wave of the energy of the ideas. The ideas themselves carried the day, while I simply served as a conduit of something I cared about. By getting out of my way, I have become a channel of the ideal of communication. It was a good trade-off.

Healing negative attitudes usually involves making such a trade. One gives up one's negative attitude by surrendering one's grip on the little self and allowing something greater to take its place. It is Cayce's simple secret, but one with profound implications for healing.

Love Conquers Fear

Cayce's general approach for dealing with something negative was to not fight it, but to replace it with a positive alternative. Quoting from the Bible (Matthew 5:39), he would advise, "Resist not evil!" It is sound psychology.

Imagine stopping a runaway horse that is galloping toward you. Would you try to fight it? Would you stand there in its path with your arms outstretched signaling for it to stop? No, because you know you would get run over. It would be better to turn and start running in the same direction as the horse's path so by the time the horse passed by, you'd have enough speed to jump on it. Then you could ride with it for a while and gradually calm it and slow it down.

It does little good to try to subdue a negative attitude by trying to knock it out, fight it back, or suppress it. Would you stop a baby from crying by covering its mouth? Negative attitudes arise from a false sense of self. They can be healed by education, by gentle leading toward a positive alternative.

Charles Thomas Cayce, Edgar Cayce's grandson, provided a good image for this process. Imagine a glass of water that is contaminated with oil. How can you get the oil out? By gentling pouring in more water, the oil is forced to the top and over the side of the glass. The water displaces the oil. It is the same way that positive attitudes can displace negative ones.

With regard to fearfulness, for example, Cayce indicated that love displaces fear. Fear is created by the illusion of separateness. It is based upon an illusion. Love is based upon the truth. The truth will dispel the illusory.

Find a way to be loving toward some aspect of a situation you fear and the fear will gradually subside. That was the principle behind Cayce's strategy for dealing with stage fright. It was also the basic strategy of those survivors of ordeals. They were in fearful situations. The natural tendency would be to try to get as far removed as possible from the situation. Instead, they found some aspect of the situation to embrace and had an experience of flow.

In my own experience, I had difficulty learning to ice-skate because I was afraid of falling on the ice. I moved rigidly and tried to stand straight up to avoid falling. I could not lean to the side to enable the edges of my skates to cut a secure path through the ice. I fought the experience every stumbling step of the way.

What was my fear? It was a concern for the safety of my body. I assumed that to fall on the ice would be the end of me. I was clinging to a limited concept of myself. I saw myself as Humpty Dumpty. My fear was convincing me that if I fell off the wall, I would not be able to get back together again.

My skating instructor kept encouraging me, "Love your edges." She demonstrated stroking the ice with the edge of her skate as she pushed off on a graceful glide. She made it look so appealing that I had to experience it myself. I leaned on the edge of my skate and pushed off into a glide. I could feel the skate's edge cutting a smooth path through the ice, making the ice almost feel as soft as ice cream. I loved the sensation.

I started making two or three strokes in a row, large steps for me, before pulling myself back upright, rigid on the ice. I needed to reassure myself that I could stand right there, in one piece. Then I pushed off again, into the wonderful sensation of a glide along the ice. Suddenly I fell. I hit the ice with a thud and slid. Momentarily I was in shock. But I was OK! I got up laughing and skated away in tears of joy! I had survived a fall. My love of gliding along the ice had freed me from my fear.

Love transports us beyond the boundaries of our separate selves and projects our attention, our caring, and our energies outward toward the focus of our love. It helps build a bridge between us and the rest of life. It delivers us from the illusion of separateness and introduces us to the truth. The truth is that we are one with life. The truth is that there is nothing to fear.

The Healing Power of Forgiveness

I have seen many people apply the formula "Love is letting go of fear" in a manner that is being cruel to themselves. They chastise themselves for being afraid. They sentence themselves to love as if they were issuing a condemnation of punishment. They struggle to love and they push away their fear, only to have their fear return the stronger. They feel defeated and guilty.

Using that formula in that way is not loving. It is instead an act of self-condemnation. Cayce warned against the evils of a judgmental attitude, whether toward another person or toward oneself. The solution is an attitude of forgiveness. It means not to blame ourselves for our limitations, but to assume that we had been doing as best we could.

When Janet, for example, came to me and told me that she blamed herself because she created her own reality, we had to get beneath the surface of that philosophy to reveal that she had not directly created that reality she called a failure. The patterns she held in her mind, her ideas, had created it.

She realized her life had been based on the feeling of being unloved and unlovable. Her father had left the family when she was a youngster. She had always wondered if it had been her fault. Perhaps she had not pleased him. She noted that her mother always seemed most loving toward her when she was pleasing her mother. From such experiences, she had formed the idea that it is important to please others if you wish to receive love.

Realistically, Janet could assume only partial responsibility for choosing to entertain such ideas about love. She needed to forgive herself, because forming such ideas were natural for a child who is totally dependent upon the love of others.

The experience of forgiveness releases our grip on anger and fear. It can heal us from negativity and make it possible to make a fresh start.

Guidance by Ideals

Adopt an attitude that is consistent with your ideal and you will invite the spiritual energy of that ideal to influence your life. The ideal will guide your actions, develop your character, and expand your awareness of spiritual states of mind.

Take good sportsmanship, for example. It is an ideal that has a long and honorable tradition. It is expressed in the attitude "It doesn't matter whether you win or lose, but how you play the game." In recent years, professional sports, and to some extent school athletics, have made a mockery of this ideal. The slogan has become "The bottom line is that winning is everything!"

The attitude expressing good sportsmanship contains an apparent contradiction that is sometimes too hard for the pressures of modern life to endure. Good sportsmanship can put you between a rock and a hard place. It's hard to be a good sport when so much is riding on winning. Not everyone can bear the strain.

Nailing yourself to the cross of contradictions, to playing your very best while not being concerned about the game's outcome, initiates you to the transcendent value of sportsmanship. You discover an extra dimension of genius in true creative play. Focusing on the process of the game rather than the outcome, you are free to focus only on the immediate moment rather than cluttering your mind with the anticipated consequences of winning or losing. y not cheating, or by not taking medicinal stimulants, you risk losing to an opponent who may not be a good sport, but you gain in other ways.

When we choose an ideal and then design optimal attitudes toward situations based on that ideal, we soon become more aware of our choices. Life becomes more intense. Your ideal will begin to guide and shape your life, but it will test you in the process.

Making a commitment to an ideal is like getting onto a roller coaster. Once you're strapped in, you're in for the duration of the ride. Negative attitudes protect us from taking risks, from getting on the roller coaster. Positive attitudes open us up to the thrill of the ride. If you can surrender to it, the ride will transport you outside yourself to an experience of exhilarating thrill!

8

Let's Get Physical

To be sure the attitudes oft influence the physical
condition of the body. No one can hate his neighbor
and not have stomach or liver trouble. One cannot
be jealous and allow anger of same and not have
upset digestion or heart disorder.
                                        Edgar Cayce 4021-1

Margaret was a very pleasant person. She had an engaging smile and reached out with her eyes to greet her visitor. She showed an interest and concern for the other person, wanting to put the person at ease. The other person was the doctor who was examining her. Margaret had shown signs of epileptic seizure, and the doctor was going to check her brain waves for signs of abnormalities. It was characteristic of Margaret that although she was the person who was in distress and who needed reassurance during this testing procedure, she was nevertheless reassuring the doctor that he needn't worry that the electrodes he was placing on her scalp might be bothering her.

The EEG record of Margaret's brain waves showed signs of irregularities. There were the telltale squiggles that indicated the presence of an epileptic condition. From this test, the doctor confirmed that Margaret indeed suffered from some form of epilepsy. The evidence was clear.

Jack was a different case entirely. He was irritable and angry as the doctor entered the examination room. He complained about having to take the brain-wave test and complained about the electrodes. He challenged the doctor's competence and was sarcastic about the value of the test. Jack talked constantly, often making off-color wisecracks. He made the doctor feel ill at ease and defensive. It was like Jack to express his nervousness in the form of aggressive teasing and snide remarks. The EEG record of Jack's brain waves showed no signs of irregularities. All the brain-wave patterns were perfectly normal. The results were as they should be, as Jack had no history of seizures. The doctor's examination confirmed that this man, although somewhat obnoxious, had a perfectly healthy brain.

Margaret was pleasant but suffered from seizures. Jack was rude and argumentative but had no signs of brain malfunction. What was perplexing was that Jack and Margaret inhabited the same body. Jack and Margaret were two different personalities of the same person. It was a case of multiple personality.

The case illustrates one of the fascinating mind-body phenomena associated with the multiple-personality disorder. The problem of multiple personality first came to public attention with the story *The Three Faces of Eve*. In recent years, therapists have discovered many similar cases and have examined them thoroughly. Multiple personalities raise a number of fascinating questions about our view of personhood. One of the most interesting are the physical aspects associated with each different personality.

Each personality inhabits the body in a different way,

creating quite noticeable differences. Each personality has a distinct tone of voice, a different set of social expressions, gestures, and postures, as well as different ways of moving about. Each is clearly a different personality, and it shows! What is surprising is the extent to which the body changes in response to the personality that is currently active.

Many details of the body's functioning are affected. In the case of Margaret and Jack, each had different brain-wave patterns. One suffered from epileptic seizures while the other did not. In other cases it's been found that different personalities show different reactions to medication. One personality is allergic to sulfa drugs, another is not. One personality suffers from asthma, while a different personality has normal breathing. One personality smokes addictively, while another is a nonsmoker. One personality is right-handed, while another is left-handed. One is so nearsighted that very strong glasses are needed to read, while another personality sees quite well with no glasses at all. Even bodily functions that would seem to be rigidly fixed by physical constraints give way to the influence of the personality.

What these cases of multiple personality show so clearly is that the body and its neurochemical functioning is under the control of the mind. The mind directs and shapes the body. Given a dramatic change in mind, there is a corresponding shift in the appearance and functioning of the body. As Cayce indicated, different attitudes create different chemical climates in the body. Our attitudes become drugs in the body. The results can be startling. The implications are immense.

We've learned how to approach the design of an ideal life. We've seen how attitude can make a difference in our experience. It's now time to get physical, to see how our attitudes affect our body, and how we can use the mind-body connection to our advantage.

Stress and Disease

Hans Selye, the originator of research on stress, coined the term, "fight-or-flight reflex." It is based on animal instinct. When something or someone threatens us, our choice is to stand and fight or to run away. Our body prepares itself for action.

Faced with a charging bear, we flush with fear. Our adrenal glands kick into gear, quickly bringing about many physical reactions. Our heart pounds harder to activate our lungs and muscles for what may ensue. The blood vessels in our fingertips and toes shrink to prevent blood loss in case of a wound. We are charged up, ready to face the grizzly opponent or run for dear life.

Whether we run away or stay and fight, our body is energized for action. When we take action, either running or fighting, we use up the adrenaline our body has produced. We get charged up with energy and we expend it. The cycle is completed. We are back to normal.

In the forest, the fight-or-flight reflex serves us well. In modern life, however, we encounter few actual bears. In today's forest, it is grizzly worries that confront us. We are never free of them.

Imagine that you are alone and helpless in a hostile world. How would you feel? Karen Horney, an eminent psychiatrist, defined *anxiety* by referring to just that very attitude. It produces its own mild fight-or-flight reflex. There are chemical consequences of anxiety within the body.

The stresses of modern life keep us in a mild state of anxiety. Anxiety keeps our adrenaline level above normal. Yet we don't actually throw spears and chase after our worries or run away on foot. We sit on our worries. We get charged up emotionally, but we do not take the vigorous action required to expend the juices and flush our system. The anxiety juices build up in our system and wear down our body. Chronic stress is bad for our health.

It was through just such an explanation that, in 1936, Hans Selye initiated the study of how stress affects the body. By the 1980s, a tremendous research explosion into the body's immune system verified much of what Cayce had described about the health consequences of attitudes. It has now become clear that mental attitude is one of the most crucial determinants of physical health.

The Mind Cures

In Charlie Chaplin's memorable movie *Modern Times*, the stresses and strains of technological life were clearly cast as the meat grinders of the human spirit. This movie made it easy to see how pressures of modern life could crush the body's ability to stay free of illness. Selye's research confirmed Chaplin's impression and helped ulcers become accepted as a physical result of psychological stress.

In later years, rumors began spreading that another form of stress played a role in disease. Lurking behind the development of cancer was the subtle culprit called grief. Hidden, unexpressed, chronic depression over a past loss was suspected as a predisposing factor in the initiation of this dread disease. As the years went by, the evidence mounted.

As it became clearer that emotional factors were involved in disease, it was also becoming clear that the mind and emotions could be involved in healing. The first "mind cures" occurred on the fringes of society. Hypnosis played a role in this early history, before the turn of the century.

Mary Baker Eddy was cured of a nervous disorder through hypnotic treatments. She later disavowed hypnosis herself and founded Christian Science. Eddy's development was but one of the several "new thought" groups formed during the turn of the century. These traditions mixed religion, positive thinking, and sometimes hypnosis into an approach to health— physical, mental, and spiritual. It wasn't until the consciousness revolution of the 1960s that their ideas began to enter into the mainstream of scientific thinking.

One of the hallmarks of the medical profession's otherwise reluctant acceptance of the role of the mind in disease and healing was the publication in 1986 of *Love, Medicine and Miracles*, by Dr. Bernie S. Siegel. Written by a Yale University surgeon, this book is a personal and professional affirmation of how the mind creates disease and how it heals it. What was most significant about this doctor's work was that he was actively practicing it himself with his patients. Using psychotherapy and other means, he helps his patients rid themselves of depression and build positive attitudes. He has taken seriously the evidence showing that attitudes such as hope, optimism, humor, and love have a curative effect upon the body's immune system. Building first upon attitudinal change, he then encourages his patients to learn the use of imagery techniques to help their bodies recover. His book is an excellent resource for seeing both the spirit and the methods of the Cayce readings on healing put into action.

After decades of research into how the mind plays a role in the creation of disease, the reverse is now as clearly established. The mind also heals.

The Physiology of the Mind

Cayce explained the relationship between attitudes and the health of the body by reference to the nervous system and the endocrine glands. He was the first psychoneuro-immunologist, presenting a holistic and integrated view of how the mind, the nervous system, and the endocrine system operate to produce health and illness. At the time of his psychic readings, his statements about the endocrine system seemed invalid. Time proved Cayce right, however, as revelations of the body's immune system became regular news items.

According to Cayce's model, we have three nervous systems. They are each associated with a different level of mind. Through a proper understanding of their functioning, however, Cayce indicated that we can gain some control over their activity.

There is the cerebral-spinal or voluntary nervous system. It controls the body's muscles and is under the voluntary control of the conscious mind. This is the nervous system that relaxes and sleeps at night. It is also the system that we can use to gain indirect control over the other systems.

There is the autonomic nervous system, controlling the functioning of the body's organs, such as the heart and digestive processes. It used to be called the involuntary system, because it seemed to function outside conscious control. Cayce, however, anticipated modern research by explaining that the autonomic nervous system, controlled by the subconscious mind, can be indirectly controlled by our attitudes and through visualization.

The autonomic nervous system contains two subsystems. One is called the sympathetic nervous system and the other is called the parasympathetic nervous system. Both respond to emotional arousal. They are like the accelerator and brake pedals of the body. The sympathetic system is the activating system. Its job is to excite the body. The parasympathetic system's job is the opposite, to calm the body. The fight-or-flight reflex is the job of the sympathetic system. Falling asleep requires the action of the parasympathetic system. The functioning of body systems is closely integrated with the functioning of the endocrine system.

Cayce identified the endocrine system as a third nervous system of its own. The endocrine system consists of the body's various glands: the pituitary, pineal, thyroid, thymus, adrenals, leydig, and gonads. Cayce indicated that this system corresponded to a series of psychic centers, known in the East as chakras. For example, the chakra name for the pineal center is the "third eye."

The superconscious mind makes its contract with the body through these psychic centers and the endocrine system. The soul's awareness, as in past-life memories and ideals, affects the physical body through this system.

Through the network of the bloodstream the endocrine glands communicate with each other and the brain through the chemicals they secrete. They also have a network of nerve fibers for communication. Taken together, the endocrine system is almost a brain unto itself. Cayce sometimes referred to it as a brain, and modern science is learning just how intelligent it is.

Research on the body's immunity response has increased our knowledge of the functioning of the endocrine system and its interaction with the autonomic nervous system. The thymus gland controls the production of the "killer cells" that fight disease. The functioning of the thymus is affected by the activities in the pineal and the adrenal glands. The activity in the adrenals is also affected by the nervous system. There are thus many different pathways by which the activity in the thymus gland can be influenced.

As neurophysiologists trace these complex paths of influence, others have discovered the truth of Cayce's major proposition about the power of the mind over the body. The essential way to influence the health and harmony within the endocrine system is through mental attitude.

The Emotional and Physical Effects of Attitude

Looking at the world through rose-colored glasses will give you a rosy disposition and a rosy complexion, too. It's about that simple, and it's true.

The attitude we assume determines the emotions we feel. Emotions have physical consequences and determine how our body functions. The creative power of attitude thus extends beyond our state of mind. Attitudes become physical.

An attitude is a frame of mind. As a perspective, it governs both what we look for and how we arrange what we see. Is your glass half empty or half full? A person with a pessimistic attitude looks at the upper part of the glass to see the empty portion. An optimist looks at the bottom part of the glass to see the full portion.

Seeing the empty portion of the glass, the pessimist feels sad. The optimist feels gratitude for what the glass still contains. Each emotional reaction is appropriate to the reality perceived. Attitude determines the nature of the reality experienced, which determines the quality of the emotional reaction.

The sadness of the pessimist is translated into physical terms. The nervous system provides a slight depressive effect. The person "loses heart" and the thymus gland responds accordingly. The immune response is weakened. Research has confirmed that loneliness, sadness, and depression weaken the immune response. Even though the glass may indeed be half empty, the pessimistic attitude is a hazard to health.

The gratitude of the optimist translates into an upbeat physical expression. Even though optimism may be unrealistic, from an objective point of view, it creates such a positive physical effect that it gives a person an edge in overcoming difficulties. Optimism is not only healthy, but also is a good strategy for coping.

Depression and Pain

Pain is a part of life. No one escapes having at least some
encounter with it. We all know what pain feels like. None of
us likes it.

Accidents and illness are occasions of actual physical
pain. Damage to the body stimulates nerve endings to send
warning signals to the brain, and we experience pain. It's a
very real, physical experience.

As physical and real as it may be, pain is also a matter of
psychology. Attitude plays a role in the creation of pain.
Research has shown that optimism and pessimism have
different effects upon the experience of pain.

Suppose you had to place your hands in a bucket of ice
water. It would hurt. How much would it hurt? It depends
upon your attitude.

People who believe that they have little or no control over
what happens to them in life find the ice water more painful
than people who believe that their own actions can make a
difference. People who are optimistic in that way experience
less pain than people who are pessimistic. Research has
proven that true, even though the optimism may have
little practical relevance to dealing with the source of
the pain.

If someone gives you a painkiller before you stick your
hand in the ice water, you will feel less pain. That would be
true even if the pill was a placebo, a phony. Expectations
and beliefs affect pain. If real pain pills are used, optimistic
people require smaller dosages to eliminate pain than do
pessimistic people.

If you are taught how to relax before sticking your hand
in the water, you will feel less pain. Relaxation can reduce
pain, but it is not the essential ingredient. As research has

shown, it is the attitude and not the actual facts that determine the subjective experience.

Using false feedback, people can be fooled to believe that they have learned the relaxation trick when, in fact, they have not. Similarly, people who have indeed learned to relax can be fooled to believe that they have not learned the trick. People who believe they have learned some control feel less pain than people who are actually relaxed but believe they have no control. Note the implications of this study: the belief of having some control has more effect on the experience of pain than does actual control.

Depression and feelings of helplessness add to the experience of pain. It is a factor in many cases of chronic pain. If the depression can be alleviated, the physical pain will also be alleviated. Alternatively, when a patient with chronic pain learns relaxation, or some other form of self-control, pain diminishes. The reduction in pain does not necessarily result from a new ability to control the source of the pain. It results as much from the release from feelings of helplessness.

The body's response to an actual, physical threat, such as something causing pain, depends upon the person's perception of the situation. Recall Cayce's advice to turn stumbling blocks into stepping-stones. His advice is based on sound physiological evidence. When the body is threatened and the person feels helpless, there are different chemical secretions in the body than if the person responds to the situation as a challenge.

Whatever the source of stress, if we can find a way to regard it as a challenge, our body will help us out. The body's ability to fight off disease, and our ability to invent creative solutions to problems, is dependent upon our taking a constructive attitude. The body is sensitive to such feelings of helplessness and such sentiments as, "I give up." Finding some way, even trivial, to believe that you can make a difference in the situation initiates a positive response within the body.

Even contemplating an upbeat approach has positive physical effects. Movies are a good way to stimulate a particular frame of mind. They can help us look on the bright side and inspire us to think positively. On the other hand, they can agitate us, incite fear, or make us feel depressed. Movies affect our body as much as our mind.

In one experiment, conducted by Harvard psychologist David McClelland, subjects viewed either a depressing movie about Nazi concentration camps or an inspiring and hopeful movie about the work of Sister Teresa. You would not be surprised to learn that afterward people who saw the first movie felt depressed while the people who saw the second movie were feeling pretty good. What might surprise you is that the chemistry in the blood of these two audiences was quite different. Blood tests revealed that the people who watched the Nazi movie left with depressed immune systems, while the people who saw the Sister Teresa movie left with their immune system strengthened.

Finding something positive to think about, reading inspirational literature, seeing a movie full of optimism, or even engaging in daydreaming about a pleasant topic can tip the scale toward a more optimistic frame of mind.

Evidence suggests that optimism actually affects the brain's preparation for pain, stimulating an increase in the secretion of natural painkillers within the bloodstream. These painkillers, called "endorphins," seem to be the body's own form of morphine. A person's state of mind has a lot to do with their production.

Pessimists are not just complainers. Their brains do not produce as much painkiller. These people have something to complain about. They can also learn how to use optimism, and other more specific skills, to make their lives more pleasant.

Modern research on pain is a good case study in appreciating the principles Cayce taught concerning how attitudes affect our body. There is a very intimate relationship between mind and body. A change in attitude has physical consequences. If a change in attitude doesn't come easily, we'll see how a minor change in behavior, applied consistently, can lead to the desired change in attitude.

Humor Medicine

We know from *Reader's Digest* that laughter is the best medicine. Cayce was also an advocate of humor. He considered it to be healthy, a sound preventative to the effects of life stress, as well as an attitude that reflected just the right approach to spiritual realities. Being able to laugh at ourselves reflects both self-acceptance and humility. It keeps the little self, the ego, in proper perspective.

The value of humor in physical healing made headlines when Norman Cousins, formerly editor of *Saturday Review*, came out with his book *Anatomy of an Illness*. There he told the story of how he cured himself of what the doctors called an incurable, terminal illness by daily doses of laughter. He watched countless hours of videotapes of old comedy shows, like Groucho Marks and the Three Stooges. He described how, after a good laugh, he felt less pain in his body. He challenged medicine to understand the mechanics of what he had accomplished. Medical research was ready to respond to the challenge.

The role of humor in the body has been suspected for a long time. Ancient Greeks viewed the functioning of the body in terms of the activities of what they called the four "humors." These were four basic bodily fluids that created corresponding temperaments—blood, phlegm, choler, and melancholy. Although the specifics of this ancient theory have been displaced by better anatomical science, the basic understanding has remained in our vocabulary. We still say that someone is in a good or ill humor, referring to their temperament. Medical science is learning just how attitudes are translated into chemical reactions within the body.

With regard to good humor, research is uncovering some of the positive effects of laughter. By showing people cartoons or comedy films, experimenters are learning about the physical side effects of laughter. They have discovered, for example, that laughter is a painkiller, as Norman Cousins observed. After viewing comedy films, subjects are much less sensitive to pain. Blood tests indicate that the immune system is stronger after a period of laughter.

Strong and hearty belly laughter is almost like exercise. It increases the rate of deep breathing and exercises the abdominal muscles. Afterward, there is a decrease in physical tension and a sense of peaceful relaxation.

Laughter can be cleansing. If you have ever experienced laughing until your side hurt and your eyes were watering, you know for yourself the sensation of having had tension washed out of your system. Laughter is clearly a tonic for stress, a purgative for the body's ills. It's what makes laughter the best medicine.

Using Physical Techniques to Improve Attitude

Being able to laugh at a time when things are not funny isn't a skill that most of us have. It would be a cruel joke if Cayce were simply to suggest that people adopt a humorous attitude at a time of crisis. He had enough compassion and understanding to know that such a suggestion would cause more harm than good. Fortunately, there is a way around this problem.

Body, mind, and spirit operate as a unit. Recall Cayce's creation principle: Spirit is the life, mind is the builder, and physical is the result. In this formula, the physical expression is at the bottom of the hierarchy. It is at the result end of the equation, not at the cause end. Thus we have explored how our ideals lead to our attitudes, which in turn affect our concrete experiences of circumstances and the operation of the body. This equation can also be reversed.

We can have our bodies perform actions that are consistent with certain attitudes. The corresponding attitude becomes easier to manifest. We can build an attitude by our bodily actions. The attitude can then take over and direct the body to produce the chemical changes consistent with that attitude.

A good case in point is the bodily reaction to panic. When a person is overcome by fear, one of the body's reactions is quickened breathing. Sometimes the fast breathing takes over to the point that the person suffers from hyperventilation. The overcharging of the system with oxygen, without the corresponding physical discharge through actual fighting or running, intensifies the panic reaction. The person becomes frozen in their steps.

One way to pull out of this nosedive into despair is to grab on to the throttle of the breath. Hold the breath momentarily and then forcefully make the breathing go slowly and deeply. Forced slow and deep breathing stops the panic reaction. It calms the person down and gives them back control over what was an out-of-control situation. Not only is the body calmed, but the panic sensation goes away. Operating on the body can affect the emotions.

When we are afraid, we can act bravely. Taking small physical steps into the face of danger, mimicking the actions of the courageous, results in small emotional changes. By acting bravely, we can come to feel more courageous. The change in attitude will translate into a chemical change in the body, giving us the energy of an uplifted and courageous heart, more stamina, and greater tolerance for pain. We can literally lift ourselves up by our bootstraps.

Actors employ this method to get into the mood of the part they are to play. They start by pretending to feel something. They act *as if* they feel it. They make faces that correspond to the mood and feeling they are supposed to enact. Researchers studying the physiological effects of actors' methods have found that the playacting does indeed bring about the physiological and chemical changes that would naturally occur if the feelings were real. These results show that actors know the secret of a "priming effect," using physical actions to create moods.

Did your parents or teachers ever suggest to you that you keep your head held high? We know moods are expressed in posture. But the reverse is also true. Postures effect mood. Walking in an upbeat, proud posture will elevate your spirits and give you a feeling of courage. Walking with your eyes to the ground, shoulders slumped, will make you feel blue.

In one study, researchers trained subjects to walk in one of two ways. In the happy gait, subjects held their head erect, swung their arms, and looked out at the horizon while they walked at a brisk pace. In the sad shuffle, subjects lowered their heads, looked at the ground, and walked in small, slow steps. At the end of the hike, those who had adopted the happy gait were feeling up and energetic. Those who had practiced the sad shuffle felt tired and blue.

It's interesting that popular speech expresses this wisdom. We'll say that life is just "getting the person down." We know what it is like to be so tired and discouraged by events that we become literally slumped over. The physical posture not only expresses but also adds to the chemical effects of our discouragement. We can give ourselves an energy boost, begin to change the chemistry in our bodies, and prepare ourselves to master the situation by simply standing tall. Walk as though you are on top of the world and you'll soon feel that way.

It's not just a way to trick yourself out of feeling bad. Walking, and exercise in general, has been found to have positive effects on elevating mood. It has been shown to be a good antidote to depression. It changes the chemistry of the body and strengthens the immune system. Besides, getting out in the fresh air and taking an enjoyable walk simply feels good.

Cayce also often recommended smiling as a way of elevating one's mood. He gave it as a formula for producing happiness when one didn't feel happy. Laboratory research has demonstrated the effectiveness of his recommendation.

In one rather unusual study, researchers manipulated by hand people's facial expression. By pushing on eyebrows and lips, they created the facial equivalents of frowns and smiles. They found that these forced masks had emotional consequences. Frowning makes people feel sad, while smiling makes them feel happy.

What if you just don't feel like smiling? What if you don't have someone who can put a smile on your face? The results of one study suggest that you can stick a pencil between your teeth and enjoy the effects of smiling. In this experiment, people looked at cartoons and rated them for humor. Some people held a pencil in their teeth, as instructed, or held a pen in their lips. Holding the pen in the lips creates a pucker that makes smile impossible, while holding the pen in the teeth forces a smile. The people with puckered mouths didn't find the cartoons very funny, while those with forces smiled were amused. Regardless of the people's intentions, the smile muscles in their face opened their hearts to humor.

If you were feeling depressed, would you be willing to stick a pencil between your teeth to force a smile? Research has proved the effectiveness of Cayce's ideas about using physical techniques to improve mood. Are you willing to have your mood lifted? It is an important question. It brings it back to you and your choices. How do you choose to feel? If you want to feel better, if you want to adopt a more constructive attitude, if you would like to feel that you can create an effect on your circumstances, there are things that you can do for yourself to prepare the way.

Cayce thus paints a picture that runs the full circle, with a place for everyone, no matter what their condition, to enter the creative process of life. You can begin by setting a spiritual ideal. Then adopt a corresponding mental attitude. Let that attitude suggest appropriate actions. The spirit thus is channeled into the physical. If things are so bad that you can't quite summon up a motivating image of your ideal, if you can't bring yourself to adopt a positive attitude, you can start with something very simple. You can find some way to act as if you felt better, you can act as if you held that constructive attitude. You can go for a walk, you can smile at someone, even though you are feeling blue. That very action will have an effect on the body to make it easier to consider adopting a more upbeat attitude; it will make it easier to envision your ideal. You can gain an edge on your situation, rekindle your belief that you can make a difference, and then take another step forward. Step by step, inch by inch, you can turn a situation around. You can survive a crisis, you can create circumstances that will help you toward having it your way.

It does require some effort. On the other hand, you are not alone. The ideal you believe in has its own power to help you. It is not a matter of your own willpower. It is more a question of whether or not you are willing to do what you can do—nothing more is asked—to allow your ideal to manifest itself in your life.

9

What Is Your Will?

The ability to choose is will; *as well as the ability to allow self to be used by influences.*
                                    Edgar Cayce, 1608-1

When Janet's husband reappeared at her doorstep, her commitment to her newly formulated ideal was tested. What was her will?

Perhaps it was because his life had not improved by ridding himself of what he considered to be an inadequate wife. Perhaps he now missed having someone else to blame for his difficulties. Whatever the reason, Janet's estranged husband returned suggesting a reconciliation.

He approached her full of apologies. The problems were all his fault, he said, and he would now be a changed man. He said he needed her to believe in him. He needed his family to inspire him toward a good life.

Janet was tempted to please him and rejoin their old marriage. Old habits do die hard. He clearly needed her. She could regain her esteem by winning his approval and praise. It was a familiar pattern. It was close at hand and easily available. He wanted her back, and she liked to be appreciated.

Although she could feel the pressure to make an immediate decision, Janet hesitated and asked for some time to think about it. She evaluated the options from the point of view of her ideal of intelligent love. She knew she needed time to regain her bearings on a new foundation in life. She accepted her desires and respected her needs.

She confessed to him that she did not have what it seemed to take to satisfy his cravings. She suggested that he enroll in an alcoholism rehabilitation program while she worked on trying to get back on her own feet. When he had achieved sobriety and was employed, and she had regained some confidence as a self-supporting woman and a working mother, then she would be willing to look at the prospects for a life together. She said she hoped it could be so. Time would tell.

Janet expressed to me her amazement at what had happened. She was surprised that she found his offer so tempting. She still loved him, and was more than willing to consider the possibility of an eventual reconciliation. She was also surprised that she had the will to counter her husband's plan with an alternative. She said that when she meditated on the feeling of intelligent love, she discovered that, more than anything else, she trusted the wisdom of respecting her need for self-confidence. She was willing to do what was necessary to get it back.

It didn't feel right to Janet to go back with her husband at this point. Janet's response to her husband's invitation, however, made her quite nervous. Wouldn't a good mother want her child to have father and mother united under one roof? What if he didn't come back a second time? Wasn't she being selfish to consider her needs over his? She suffered many anxieties as a result of her idealistic decision, but she was also excited at the prospects of a new life. She had no guarantees that it would work out. All she had to hold on to was that her decision felt right when viewed from the spirit of her ideal. She was willing to be guided by that feeling.

An Alternative to Willpower

You can choose your ideal; you can have it your way. But, like Janet, you may have to face the question of whether you are willing to have things as you choose. Cayce paints a pretty optimistic picture about the possibilities that are available to you when you build upon an ideal with the powers of the mind. It may sound good but feel unrealistic. It depends on what you are *willing*.

It's easy to say: pick an ideal, design your attitudes to keep them positive, and take a walk when you are feeling blue. It's easy to say, but not easy to do. It seems like we are talking about a heroic amount of willpower. It seems like a lot of work. When we are depressed, feeling blue, or even tired, or when we are sick, frightened, or overwhelmed, who needs help in the form of making greater effort? What if you can't bring yourself to smile when you're depressed? Anyone who says you can always do as you choose just hasn't been in any tough situations.

To believe that you can do anything you choose also sounds somewhat grandiose. It doesn't seem right somehow that by sheer strength of will you can expect to always have things your way. It seems selfish and manipulative. It also sounds a bit deluded. It's one thing to accept that faith can move mountains, but it would seem that greed could only destroy a mountain.

The Cayce readings offer a perspective on will that helps

us get around both the willpower trap and the evil of
self-centered willfulness.

Studying the problem of healing negative attitudes, we
saw that it did little good to try to beat down the negative. It
required, instead, supplanting the negative with a positive
alternative. Similarly, relying on raw willpower is often
counterproductive. Tapping into a higher form of will will
prove to be a better strategy. Relating to a higher will, first
expressed in the form of an ideal, also helps guide our
behavior according to spiritual values and leads us to the use
of higher powers of the mind.

Qualities of the Will

Hidden in the shadows, behind the superhero willpower,
the true will is the dynamic, propelling force of every soul.
Cayce viewed the will as one of the three dimensions of the
soul, along with spirit and mind. In *Paradox of Power:
alancing Personal and Higher Will*, Mark Thurston provides an in-depth discussion of Cayce's perspective on the
will. Examining the many times Cayce referred to the
activity of the will, Thurston found that it had nine essential
qualities.

The will is the *chooser*. Souls have the same free will as
their Creator. It is a freedom of choice. Among the various
patterns the mind generates, the will can choose the one
upon which to focus attention. The path of attention, in fact,
is a good place to watch the footprints of the will. Our
attention follows our will. When the will is inactive, our
attention and our behavior follow the path of habits. When
the will is active, we become more aware of our choices and
more in touch with our reality as creative souls.

The will is the *active principle* within the soul. The spirit
dimension of the soul is pure energy, without pattern or

direction. The mind patterns the energy while the will directs it. It is the will that provides the soul with its impetus for growth and evolution. Without the will, the mind's past patterns completely determine the manifestation of spirit. When this active principle is dormant, or hidden, our actions appear to be the passive follower of habit or mood.

The will is the *motivator.* That is the quality of the will that helps us take initiative. It gets us moving in a particular direction. It channels our energy into action. When the will is dormant, it becomes hard to take action on our wants. We are stuck in the daydreaming, wishing stage of living. We are full of good intentions, but can't seem to start anything.

The will is the *changer.* It is the will that stops us in a chain of thought and says, "Hold on here! I don't have to think this way!" Mental patterns have a life of their own, following the rules of the mind. It is the will that can give the mind a turn and steer it in a new direction. It is the ability of the will to release us from the grip of a particular mental pattern. When the will is active, it can change our habits. Cayce indicates that it is the will that frees us from our past.

The will is the *developer.* While the patterns of the mind are governed by the past, the will is directed toward the future. The mind knows patterns; the will knows objectives. While the mind may shift from one pattern to the next, the will holds to a particular pattern and perseveres to the completion of the goal. Whereas the mind is easily bored with repetitious stimulation, the will has the patience to remain focused until it meets its objective.

The will is the *individualizer.* It is what distinguishes our individuality, our true self, from our personality. Much of our personality is learned, and represents only a certain surface part of our being. During the course of a lifetime, we are presented with thousands upon thousands of choices.

Each choice takes us down a different road. The sum total of our choices is our individual path.

The will is our *guide*. How can we choose among the patterns in the mind without some basis of selection? The will guides the choices. The will can also direct the creative function of the mind. Once it is awakened, the will is a source of guidance that we can turn to for help and direction.

The will is also the *agent of obedience*. It is that part of us that is *willing* to be subject to influence. The will is what makes it possible for us to be guided by influences beyond the individual self. It can open us to the influence of the spiritual forces contained in ideals.

Finally, the will exists in *opposition to the mind*. Many of the qualities of the will that we have discussed involve some kind of opposition to the mind. The will can oppose the habits of the mind, it can oppose the momentum of the mind, and it can reactivate the inertia of the mind. Most of the time that we speak of willpower, in fact, we are talking about the struggle of the conscious mind to oppose or control the activity of the will. Willpower is the domain of the conscious mind. It is a counterfeit will. Willpower is the creation of the conscious mind to make up for the loss of contact with the true will. To learn to awaken the authentic will, we will need to go deeper than the workings of conscious mind.

The Physical Will

Will is an active principle. It is dynamic. It is physical. Getting our body to move as we wish is the first place we experience the will in action. Our eyes and head move with our attention. Our arms reach out to what attracts our interest. We crawl and then we walk. As body coordination develops, we are able to express more of our will through physical action.

As adults, our bodies express our will without our thinking about it. Bodily movement becomes so automatic that we take it for granted. Only when trying to develop a new skill, or when confronted by injury or infirmity, do we realize that our will and our bodily motions are not automatically one and the same thing. Learning to dance ballet, to play golf or tennis, or to finger a guitar, we have to become more intimately aware of how the body moves to be able to express our will in action. Under ordinary circumstances, however, our bodies are controlled through an unconscious will rather than through conscious willpower.

Operating outside of conscious awareness, the will directs the life force of the human being. Cayce indicates that the spiritual level of the will acts through the throat chakra, corresponding to the thyroid gland. One of the main purposes of the thyroid is to regulate metabolism, the energy-combustion process of the body. As we learned in the last chapter, the glands of the endocrine system communicate with one another and with the nervous system. Thus, the activity in the thyroid affects and is affected by activity in other regions of the body.

The autonomic nervous system, under the control of the subconscious mind, regulates the body's machinery. Here is another aspect of the functioning of the will. It is the body's will to have the heart beat and the lungs breathe, to digest food and metabolize it as energy for the body's use. The very will to live plays an important role in health and in the recovery from illness.

The will to live is expressed in instincts, reflexes, and appetites. The survival of the body is dependent upon the functioning of the will at this basic physical level. Jerking our hand away from a hot stove and blinking our eyes when objects approach them are both critical to survival. As the body is depleted of water or food, we automatically develop feelings of thirst or hunger. The regulation of eating and drinking is an automatic process governed by the healthy functioning of the will.

Appetites are one place that we can see how distortions to the body's chemistry play havoc with the healthy will. As an extreme case, mice given a choice between food, water, and cocaine will very soon opt only for cocaine. Forsaking food and water for this drug, they will consume cocaine to the point of a very premature death. People who have developed drug addictions will demonstrate similarly self-destructive behaviors. Addictions are an obvious example of how a chemical effect within the body can kidnap a person's will, holding the person hostage to a craving.

As in any hostage situation, addictions gain their power by applying leverage to the body's will toward survival. Addictive cravings actually express, in a distorted manner, the body's inner wisdom. When we ingest a drug, or overeat, the body attempts to compensate in order to regulate an internal balance. With continued ingestion of that substance, the body habituates to the chemical additives and calculates it into its balance sheet. The result is that when the ingestion doesn't occur, the body misses it. The body would gradually return to a normal balance, but the craving experienced in the meantime stimulates the person to ingest more. Thus an addiction is formed.

Edgar Cayce took this compensatory physical process into account when giving suggestions for how to overcome addictions. He interpreted the cravings as a chemical process expressive of the body's now distorted will. He didn't suggest fighting that will, but reshaping it. He gave prescriptions for alternative substances to ingest, to help the body adjust to the withdrawal of the addictive substance. To people with overeating problems, he suggested taking a glass of water with four to six ounces of grape juice before meals to curb the appetite. For alcoholics, depending upon the individual, he recommended gold chloride mixed in water with bromide of soda. For some smokers, he suggested the vegetable salsify. Other suggestions can be found in Reba Ann Karp's *Edgar Cayce: Encyclopedia of Healing*.

We express through a body and we are dependent upon a healthy body to be able to have our will function in harmony with our purposes. Sufficient exercise, a well-balanced diet, and a minimal intake of addictively reacting substances (sugar, coffee, alcohol, salt, tobacco) help ensure that the body's will is not diverted away from its mission. Abuse of the body in these areas sidetracks the will into the task of counterbalancing our self-destructive actions. This same principle can be seen in other disturbances of the will, where Cayce's approach to healing—supplanting the negative with a positive—remains the formula for regaining harmony with oneself. Healthy habits and appetites can be cultivated in the same way as positive attitudes.

Will in Conflict

Joe was always late. He was late for work, for his appointments, for dates. He joked that he was even late for his own birth, as it was a delayed delivery. Although he joked about it, Joe seemed quite upset about his habitual tardiness, for it brought him a lot of grief.

His co-workers were annoyed with him. He had lost credibility with his friends. He tried many different strategies to learn to be on time. He even got himself a watch. He maintained a written schedule of activities and wrote himself notes. No matter what he seemed to try, it didn't work. His work supervisor was understandably concerned about the problem. After repeated attempts to work with Joe on a solution, he suggested that Joe get some counseling.

Joe presented himself to me as an abject failure. He had developed a shamedog manner because he was always apologizing. He was obviously hurt by the frowns he received. He wanted to please other people. He had many commitments, he made many promises, but kept only a few. He was ashamed of how he so frequently disappointed other people. He appeared to be a person who was totally out of control. Joe was hoping that I could help him make his willpower more effective so he could straighten up his life.

Joe was a typical workaholic, attempting to do more than he was capable, working on several tasks at once, and always in a hurry. Not only was he tardy, but he was constantly behind schedule. Besides his regular job, he had a part-time job and ran a business on the side. He had little time for himself and seemed to derive little satisfaction from his life.

The more I learned about Joe, however, the more I suspected that his life was more under control than he cared to admit. Joe's predictable tardiness appeared to be a compensation for his apparent lack of control. He didn't know how to say no, to turn down an assignment, but he did know how to be late. Being late was his say of saying no. It was his way of protesting the hurriedness of his life. It was his inner nature in rebellion. Without the tardiness factor, what would keep Joe from spinning wildly into oblivion? Being behind on his work was Joe's way of controlling his schedule.

Joe didn't have the will to control his life, because it would mean he would have to assume responsibility for his choices. He couldn't please everyone, and someone would be angry at him for not choosing in their direction. Joe's hectic schedule took the blame rather than Joe himself. His tardiness was something that people tried to help him with, and people learned to make allowances for it. He was afraid he wouldn't get that kind of understanding and support if he were to stand up and declare, ''I don't want to do this or

that, and I'm not going to do it." Instead, he paid lip
service to wanting to accomplish so much and to being a
team player. He was *trying* to be on time; he was *trying* to
get his jobs done on schedule.

Joe wasn't aware of his secret feelings of resentment. He
wasn't aware that he was being late on purpose as a form of
protest. He sincerely believed that he was trying to exert his
willpower to getting himself places on time and his work
done on schedule. During our counseling sessions, he became aware of his feelings of resentment and rebellion. It
was a secret part of himself that he didn't want revealed. He
felt more comfortable resisting it, fighting it, and condemning
it. His willpower was on the side of his public self—the
diligent, overscheduled worker. His will, however, was on
the side of the tired, neglected, rejected self.

I had Joe practice claiming his will. I asked him to affirm
his "bad" behaviors, saying to himself, but not necessarily
to others, that he was late on purpose. He was then to ask
himself what his purpose was. In that way, he learned to
thank that rebel part of himself, for it was the only part that
actually stood up for his feelings. He wouldn't do that for
himself. He learned that this secret part had a more intuitive
reaction to events, whereas Joe's conscious reaction to
things was always to think about them endlessly. What he
called his lazy self was actually more gifted in ways than
Joe. It had a lot to offer. His rebel part taught him how he
felt inside. It was also the seat of his will, and its strength
was more powerful than Joe's conscious willpower.

Our counseling work involved his learning to respect his
secret self and to listen to its advice. He had to learn to
make allowances for his needs for time out, for a more
balanced approach to living. He found it hard to go public
with his desire to work less, but gradually he found ways to
do so. Finally, he was able to quit his part-time job and let
his business go. He had less money, but he had more time

for himself. He refound his enthusiasm for arts and crafts and returned to his pastime of going to the movies. He was much happier. At his regular job, he was now on time and caught up in his work. He soon received a substantial promotion, with a salary increase that more than made up for the lost income from his part-time job.

Joe now felt much more in control of his life. He also felt more in touch with himself. Learning to listen to that secret part of himself became listening to that still-small voice within. He was now in touch with an inspiring source of guidance from within his being. At times, he had to assert his independence from its advice. He found that it took a lot of willpower, however, to fight his inner will. He began to discover that it wasn't worth the effort. When he was willing to follow the inner voice, his life went so much more smoothly. He had discovered the power and the peace that comes from being in harmony with his true will.

Joe's story has something to teach us all. Very often the very symptoms or habits that we are trying to change by strength of willpower are in fact expressive of our will. It is a will that is unconscious because we are unconscious of our true feelings. Willpower is often what the conscious mind substitutes for actual will when it is only the conscious mind that wants something.

It usually pays to look at the symptom, to ask it what will it is expressing. It is the principle of *resisting not evil*, looking instead for the purpose behind the symptom, the need it is serving. When the need is known, a more constructive manner of meeting that need can be found. This procedure also puts the conscious mind more in harmony with the truer will, where they can cooperate to bring about better results.

As Joe found, being in touch with the inner will also brings the advantage of an intuitive guidance. Will is not only a motivator but also a source of guidance. If the conscious mind is overly dominant with its willpower, this source of guidance from the will is usually hidden. It can be hidden behind a symptom, a certain laziness or resistance to doing things demanded by the willpower. If the conscious mind is willing to surrender its control and listen, the voice of the will can speak.

The Experience of Willingness

Very little of our will originates from within our conscious mind. It can be made conscious, but to do so requires honest self-evaluation and learning the freedom that comes from surrendering to one's true nature as a spiritual being. The conscious mind has to let go of willpower as its model of the will and adopt a model based more on willingness.

The experience of willingness is the closest approximation the conscious mind can get, at first, to the experience of will. Willingness would seem like the opposite of will, especially if willpower is held as the standard. Willpower seems like strength, while willingness seems like weakness. There is strength in true will, a strength similar to that we associate with conscious willpower, but its best representation in the conscious mind is the experience of willingness.

When we say, "I am willing to do whatever is necessary to . . ." we are expressing true will. When we make such a statement, we are confessing that our choice of direction or goal is coming from a place of deep decision. Our resultant actions almost feel involuntary, for we have no choice but to act as we do. That compelling quality is the action of the will. It is a different feeling than willpower.

The exercise of willpower brings with it the feeling of effort in the overcoming of resistance, while the expression of will has more the feeling of determination. Using willpower requires us to continue to decide in its favor. Each moment is a temptation to give in to impulse and let go of willpower. The expression of authentic will, however, doesn't ask us to keep making a decision in its favor. The decision feels locked in place.

Most of us can distinguish between those times where we have to continue to invoke willpower and those situations where our authentic will is active and we are its willing servant. The first situation becomes quickly tiring. The second situation feels like we are "in for the ride." The decision carries us along. From the standpoint of the conscious mind, an act of will is somewhat like a voluntary surrender to a choice so that what follows is more like an involuntary going along. Willingness is a voluntary act that leads to involuntary compliance with the will. One does what must be done.

The Willingness to Surrender to a Higher Power

People who have come to moments of decision in their lives and have had experiences of will find that same sense of freedom. It requires no effort to carry out the decision. It is not a struggle. Willpower is not involved. One is simply willing to do what is necessary.

It is not surprising that religious conversions often involve such acts of will. When alcoholics experience turning their drinking problem over to their higher power, they discover a relief from not having to struggle with the issue. It is over. A higher will was invoked and took the issue out of their hands.

I can testify to this effect. The first step in my recovery from alcoholism was the experience of realizing I was not willing to stop drinking. Most of us alcoholics maintain that we are in control. It took a particularly bad experience for me to recognize that I loved drinking so much that I would never voluntarily stop. I know I was sincere in what I said, because I was terrified at the admission. It was like having my fate sealed. I was truly despairing. There I became in touch with my true will.

Later, I became aware of why I was willing to do anything necessary to have my drinks. Alcohism is truly a questing after spirit. Feeling relaxed, feeling in the flow, through drinking I was able to give way to the river of life. Yet it was not a true surrender to the flow of life. I maintained control. I kept the genie in the bottle. I would uncork it when I wanted the experience of flow. Afterward, I would return to my normal state of consciousness. I wanted access to the experience of flow on my own terms. I wanted the power to control the flow.

Alcohol, however, was controlling my life. I attended meetings of Alcoholics Anonymous. I accepted the fact that I was an alcoholic. My personal story was not unique to me; my story was the story of alcohol—all such stories are essentially the same. I was possessed by a spirit that took advantage of my need for power. As long as I insisted on my being in control, I would continue to be possessed by the alcoholic spirit. It was a sobering realization.

It was also freeing to realize that if I was willing to surrender my need for personal control, I could invite a higher power to pattern my life. It could displace the power that alcohol had over me. I didn't know how to act on that realization. All I could do was to imagine what it might be like and wait.

One day I found that I could no longer drink. When I went to the liquor store that afternoon and reached for a bottle, I found I was hesitating. I didn't understand what I felt, but I felt it clearly: drinking was no longer an option.

As I left the store empty-handed, I wondered what was going on. Had my higher power taken the decision out of my hands? I hadn't made a decision to stop drinking. I felt some sadness at the loss. Even though it seemed that I had no choice in the matter, I accepted it. I was willing not to drink. Never did I experience, since that moment, having to use any willpower not to drink. That is the freedom granted by the willingness to be guided by a higher power of will.

Later I learned a clue about my participation in the action of my higher power. Browsing through my dream journal, I found a dream that preceded by a few days the cessation of drinking. In this dream I found a bottle of whiskey in a cabinet and threw it away. That dream may have reflected the soul's decision to quit.

Although the drinking stopped, the quest after spirit did not. My own case is but another of those examples of a spiritual journey initiated by a personal crisis. My will toward spirit was redirected from a destructive approach to a more constructive search for inner freedom and peace through dream study, therapy, meditation, and the application of the gifts of the spirit in my family and social and work relationships. I will always be thankful that my experience with alcoholism directed me to the secret of surrender to a higher power.

Imagination and the Will

Invoking our higher will is the surrender to guidance from our ideals. It is important that we are able to visualize our ideal so vividly that the ideal is compelling. When the ideal is compelling, we can surrender to it. We accept it and are willing to do what is necessary to stay in harmony with that ideal.

An ideal then becomes like an ark. It is something that you can hang on to; its power becomes your power. It is a lot better than gritting your teeth trying to do right.

If you make a tight fist and hold it until your arm gets

tired and sore, and then try to hold the fist a bit longer, where is the will? The decision to keep your fist clenched is an act of conscious willpower. The aching along the back of your hand is the expression of the will, asking that the tension be released. Holding the fist clenched is a voluntary act, while the aching is involuntary. The willpower to keep the fist closed requires your continuing to decide to keep exerting that effort.

Now imagine that you are holding something very precious in your hand, but someone wants to rob you of it, to pluck it out of your hand. Try to imagine this situation as vividly as you can. The robber pries at your fingers to force you to let go of your fist. The prospect of having your valuable belonging stolen horrifies you, and you hold fast. Your fist clamps shut like an iron lock. The clenching of the fist is now almost involuntary. You can't help but hold back from the efforts of the thief. The aching along the back of your fist doesn't feel quite the same as it did before. Instead of a pleading ache, it feels more like the strength of your determination. You are willing to keep your fist clenched as long as necessary until the thief gives up. The power to keep your fist closed comes from the compelling value of what you are holding on to, not from your conscious willpower.

This example illustrates an important secret about the will, the imagination, and the hidden powers of the mind. We will be discussing these powers in the next section of the book, where it will be helpful to you to be familiar with how to access your higher will through the willingness to imagine.

In our example, by the use of the imagination, you were able to invoke your will. By imagining that you were holding something valuable in your hand and that someone was trying to steal it, your will automatically determined to keep your hand closed. Your imagination created a reality and your will responded accordingly in an automatic fash-

ion. You did not have to decide, or use willpower, to keep
your hand closed.

Finally, note that as you imagined your hand holding
something valuable, it was your will that was active in
clenching your fist, while your role was the more passive
one of being *willing* to hold your fist as long as necessary.
We mentioned earlier that willingness is the conscious
equivalent of the expression of the true will. The use of the
imagination plus willingness will be the key to learning to
invoke your will to accomplish things that you could not do
through conscious willpower. In the next chapter, for example, you will learn how to create an effect in your body by
imagining the effect and then being willing for the effect to
occur. Imagining something, and then being willing to allow
what you imagine to be true, is the secret of invoking your
will.

Besides through the functioning of our body and through
our actions, our will expresses itself through the imagination. Every day we spontaneously have daydreams. We do
not plan to have them. They occur involuntarily. What
comes to your imagination involuntarily is an expression of
your inner will. One way to come to know the direction of
your will is to listen to your imagination. It can be a form of
meditation, or a mode of self-exploration.

There is a subtle interplay between our conscious willpower, the inner will, and the imagination. The imagination
is a place where your conscious willpower and your inner
will can dialogue. You can use conscious willpower, for
example, to initiate a sequence in the imagination.

Think of two different animals, for example. What animals came to your mind? You consciously commanded
yourself to think of animals, and your imagination com-
plied. Yet the particular animals that came to mind were a
spontaneous expression of your inner will.

Conscious willpower can initiate a sequence in the imagination, but it is of limited value in directing the sequence. Your will also gives direction to your imagination. Two forces collide: what you consciously decide to imagine and what your will imagines. As you explore this phenomenon, you will learn that an attitude of willingness is the way to coax your will to imagine what your conscious mind directs.

Think of your two animals again and have them interact. Make them do things together that you decide for them to do. Have them get along the way you want them to. See how much control you have over their actions.

How were you as an animal trainer? If you are like most people, you found that you could get them to do most of what you thought to command them to do. How did you decide what commands to give? Was it a conscious, deliberate decision, or did certain thoughts just come to you? It's a hard question to answer. You probably also found that not everything you commanded was performed with the same vividness in your imagination. Some things you could easily see, and others were more vague and more like thoughts.

Whatever it is that your inner will wants to imagine, the more vividly you will see it and the more spontaneity it will have. The vividness of your imagination is also a function of the degree to which your willingness matches your will, because you can otherwise try to distract your attention away from your imagination. The more willing you are to imagine what is in your heart, the more vividly you will see it in your mind's eye.

Shaping the Will With an Ideal

In our example of the clenched fist, it was the power of values, or ideals, that guided the functioning of the will's power. The action of your will to keep your hand closed was determined by the fact that you were valuing what you held in your hand. When you imagine an ideal so vividly that it is real for you, your will automatically guides your actions to be in accord with the values expressed in that ideal.

By imagining your ideal, you can shape your will. At first, your will may not be in accord with your ideal. As you examine your actions, you may find they express a contrary will. You can try to imagine an ideal alternative, but you may find your imagination spontaneously presenting some contrary images, expressive of your contrary will. It isn't effective to try to force your imagination, through willpower, to comply with your ideal.

When willpower and the imagination are pitted against one another, the imagination wins because it expresses the inner will. The conscious mind does have some input, and can coax the imagination of the inner will. With your conscious will you can decide what to imagine, but then you have to switch over to the seemingly passive willingness. As you are then willing to surrender to the imagination, your will may assent to your expectation, or it may modify it with something of its own.

When Janet's husband asked to return, Janet tried to visualize her ideal of intelligent love. For a while, however, her imagination came up with images of being alone and afraid. We did not try to force the issue, but instead examined the meaning of her frightening images, for they were the authentic expression of her will at that moment. We realized that her will was responding to the eruption of her habitual idea that one needs to please others in order to be loved and secure.

Janet began to feel angry about being kept hostage to that false notion. Her anger was the expression of her will to be free, to be herself. I asked her if she was willing to love herself no matter what, for that would be necessary to break free. She said she was willing, but didn't know if she could. I suggested that she forget about the situation with her husband for a moment and get into the mood of her ideal of intelligent love. As she did so, I asked her to experience herself from that perspective. I asked her to imagine what she might do with the habitual notion that she needed to please others in order to be loved. She saw herself taking herself by the hand, turning away from that notion, and embracing herself. She started to cry. She could indeed love herself, and it freed her from her fears.

Discussing this experience, Janet expressed some relief to discover that it simply felt better to love herself than to be afraid about pleasing others. That discovery made it easier for her, because she was certainly willing to feel better. Now when she tried to visualize her ideal of intelligent love and view the situation with her husband, her will spontaneously expressed in imagination her confessing to her husband that she just couldn't get back together with him at that time.

Janet's experience shows how the inner will cannot be forced but can be developed and shaped. It required that she know her ideal and that she engage in some honest self-evaluation of her feelings. She was then able to forgive herself for harboring the false notions that created her fearful attitude. When she ceased condemning herself, she was able to redirect her will toward her ideal, and her imagination now expressed her single-mindedness of intention.

Authentic will, approached not through willpower but through willingness to be influenced by an ideal, stands at the threshold between the use of the conscious mind in the ways we have explored in this section of the book (setting an ideal, working with attitudes, and taking physical actions) and the use of the hidden powers of the mind, as in creative visualization, self-hypnosis, and autosuggestion. It is through these hidden reserves that we can develop and apply the will to create an ideal life.

PART III

Hidden Powers of the Mind

Meditation, hypnosis, trance, deep relaxation, reverie, visualization, and suggestion—these are some of the more dramatic phenomena associated with the mysteries of the mind. Perhaps it was an interest in one of these altered states of consciousness that originally attracted you to this book. We are going to deal with these things now and we are going to learn how to use them.

In Part One, we learned about Cayce's metaphysical perspective on the mind. We learned that the mind is a reality that transcends individual persons. We also learned that the mind exists in levels of reality that are normally outside our awareness, in the subconscious and universal unconscious regions. We are about to learn how to contact those levels of the mind.

We have learned how God exists in this world as spirit, mind, and will. As creations of God, as souls, we too share in having these three dimensions of being. We learned Cayce's formula for creation: The spirit is the life force. It is pure energy. Mind, called "the builder," is what gives energy its patterns. The will chooses the mental pattern that the energy then shines through, creating the visible forms of matter. That is the process of creation. As souls, we are co-creators with God of reality.

In Part Two, we applied Cayce's metaphysical formula of creation to the matter of daily life. First we faced the fact that experience is subjective, that our expectations do get fulfilled. We learned that it is more true to say that we see what we believe than to say that we believe what we see. That realization posed a problem. If life is a dream, then how do you decide what dream to have? Cayce's answer to that question is that it is important that you begin the process of conscious creation by deciding upon your spiritual ideal. What is your highest value, what is your vision of the Ultimate Good, that you would use to guide your life? We modified the slogan of the New Age, "You create your own reality," to a more accurate statement: the ideas you adhere to create your reality. Following the formula for creation, spirit-mind-physical, in daily life led to the sequence: ideal, attitude, action. Choose an attitude that is consistent with your ideal, then act as dictated by that attitude. We learned that the development of the will was important in being able to discipline the spontaneity and freewheeling aspect of the mind so that we keep our attention on the desired mental patterns.

In Part Three, we will continue with the theme that has been presented and now bring an extra dimension of power to the formula for creation. Knowing the metaphysics of creation and the important role of the mind, knowing the vital importance of ideals and attitudes in domesticating these metaphysical truths, we are now ready to begin to use the deeper powers of the mind that are hidden within altered states of consciousness.

We have more than the conscious mind to use in our efforts to apply the spirit (ideal), mind (attitude), physical (action) formula to creating our life. We have the hidden powers of the subconscious and the universal unconscious mind. We will begin by learning about the nature of altered states of consciousness, how to meditate, what happens when we fall asleep, and the value of dreams. Then we will learn about deep relaxation and how to open ourselves to the creative powers of the subconscious.

Knowing how to drop down to these deeper regions, we will learn about the importance of mental imagery, expressed both as the visionary capabilities of the imagination and the creative power of visualization. We will then learn how to combine the power of visualization and the power of suggestion to train the subconscious mind to help us in our quest to manifest our ideals.

By learning to explore the unconscious in a manner that is designed to help us and bring good into the world, we can feel more comfortable about our explorations of these deeper mysteries of the mind. In learning how to create our own ideal life, we can also learn how to channel the spiritual wisdom of our higher self. In so doing, we become co-creators with God, thus fulfilling the spiritual purpose of our being.

10

Altered States of Consciousness

In deep meditation there descends the influences to open the channels . . . to the inmost recesses of the Creative Forces in body.

Edgar Cayce 275-39

You see lying before you a woman reading a book. Suddenly, as she gets up, the space between you and her is disrupted and distorted. As she swims away, you realize that all this time you have been looking through water at a woman under water.

This description is of a visually stunning television commercial advertising a pool cleaner. The idea is that it cleans the water so perfectly clear, you don't even know the water is there. The water is invisible until it begins to move.

This scene is an instructive analogy to the mind and consciousness. When the mind is steady and clear, we don't notice its presence. We see the world directly, our vision passing right through an invisible, transparent mind. But when our consciousness is altered, when the mind is no

longer steady and clear, the ripples awaken us to the mind's
existence. Thus, the psychedelic drug movement of the 1960s
earned its name. Psychedelic means "mind-manifesting."
By dramatically altering consciousness, these drugs revealed
the creative presence of the mind in all we experience. It
was part of the beginnings of the consciousness revolution.

Altered states of consciousness do not have to imply such
risky and dubious activities as drug use. Every day we alter
our consciousness as we go to sleep. We can begin with this
normal psychedelic trip to learn to explore other altered
states that we can use to our advantage.

Sleep: The Daily Psychedelic Trip

What happens when we fall asleep at night? Have you
ever stayed up to watch? Cayce indicated that doing so
would be very instructive. There is a lot to learn from
staying awake while you fall asleep.

That we say "falling asleep" or "drift off to sleep" is
revealing of what we understand about the process. The first
step, Cayce notes, is that we withdraw our attention from
the external world. As our eyes and ears shut down, we
ignore the external world. The inner world of our own
thoughts becomes our reality.

The story *Alice in Wonderland* begins with Alice falling
asleep as her sister reads to her. As she goes to sleep, she no
longer hears what her sister is reading. Instead, she falls
into a hole in pursuit of a rabbit.

I'm sure you've had a similar experience. Perhaps while
watching TV you have drifted off to sleep momentarily.
Awakening, you realize you must have been asleep because
you have lost track of the TV show. Only moments ago you
were experiencing something else, you were somewhere
else, but you didn't suspect you were asleep.

As we relax the body and the physical senses, Cayce explained, the conscious mind begins to shut down. The conscious mind is dependent upon the activity of our senses. As the conscious mind shuts down, the subconscious mind emerges as our consciousness. Here we have a normal, everyday, but very significant altered state of consciousness. The altered consciousness of the presleep state is subconsciousness.

Falling or drifting, as we go to sleep, the conscious mind surrenders its existence by letting its senses shut down. Our attention drifts with the stream of thought into the upper regions of the subconscious mind. One of the things that happens is that our thoughts become more visual. If the conscious mind thinks with words, the subconscious mind thinks with pictures. As the sun sets, words disappear and the pictures within us become more visible.

We begin to imagine scenes. If we were awake, we would realize we were daydreaming. We would know where we were, and that the pictures in the mind were just that—pictures in the mind. But as we fall into the subconscious, we take these mental pictures to be our reality. It is jarring to wake up suddenly and realize that although we thought we were awake and visiting with a friend, we were actually falling asleep into a daydream.

Falling into a daydream is an important part of the process of falling asleep. It gives our fading consciousness something to hold on to, like a security blanket. The images that come to us as we fall asleep distract our attention from the process of falling asleep. The conscious mind needs to be lulled asleep.

As we continue to fall asleep, our consciousness alters further. Very few of us are able to stay awake this far into the journey toward deep sleep and dreaming. Through his psychic trance, Cayce was able to describe what happens.

The conscious mind and its sensory system collapses down to a single sense. Cayce calls it a "sixth sense" and describes it as most closely resembling hearing. We fall into a state of listening. It is not an ordinary listening, but a cosmic resonance to universal vibrations. It is as if our individual being dissolves back into its source. All that remains is listening. It is a state of psychic union with all of life. It is a state of pure intuition.

Deep sleep is such a dark and remote state of unconsciousness that it's hard to believe any awareness could exist there. But there is evidence that we do listen while we sleep. I'm not referring to the fact that our baby's cry will wake us up while we will sleep through the sounds of traffic. This everyday phenomenon suggests that we are always listening, ignoring innocent sounds, but are ready to get up at the sound of trouble. Instead, what I'm referring to is the recent revelation that patients under heavy anesthesia are often able to hear the conversations of the operating staff during surgery. Doctors were resistant to the evidence for a long time, because it violated both common sense and traditional medical thought. But now, a newsletter devoted to educating surgeons about the implications of this surprising revelation, "Human Aspects of Anaesthesia," suggests that every operating room contain a sign reading, "Be careful, the patient is listening."

The conscious mind considers deep sleep a void of utter darkness, but the unconscious mind finds it full of life. Cayce described sleep as a "shadow of, that intermission in earth's experiences of, that state called death." Falling asleep is like dying. We give up the world and our control over it to surrender to a dark unknown. From the perspective of the conscious mind, we cease to be. But like death, sleep is not a termination of existence, but a transformation of existence into the realm of the unconscious. We fall asleep, but awaken into a dream.

What Is a Dream?

Going to sleep is a night sea journey. On this trip, we encounter an island of light. As the subconscious mind takes the helm normally held by the conscious mind, the soul awakens. The soul is actively conscious, Cayce indicates, only when the conscious mind is laid aside and the subconscious mind becomes the consciousness.

We are sleeping on our portion of universal awareness. It lies dormant within us until we are asleep. The soul brings its own light to our darkness and peers about in our dreams.

A dream is an experience the soul has while we are asleep. With its universal awareness its reach for information knows no bounds. It remembers all its past lives, the lessons learned, as well as the purpose for incarnating this lifetime. It looks upon our daily activities and our experiences and views them in the context of its ageless wisdom. Knowing that a dream is an experience of the soul makes it easy to understand the source of the extraordinary phenomena that happen in dreams.

Dreams have been the most frequent source of psychic experiences. On the one hand, surveys have shown that people who have had psychic experiences (telepathy, contact with the dead, seeing the future) indicate that dreams were the most frequent source of these experiences. On the other hand, laboratory investigations attempting to demonstrate the reality of ESP have found dreams to be the most reliable state of consciousness for producing verifiable telepathic events. Psychic dreams can be understood as resulting from the soul's reach beyond time and space.

Most religions can trace their origins to dreams. Besides the dreams heralding the birth of Jesus, dreams also figured in the birth of Buddhism and Mohammedism. The autobiographies of religious leaders and mystics often contain stories of special dreams of spiritual significance. It is common for people who meditate on spiritual matters or lead an active prayer life to have dreams concerning religious themes. Religious dreams can be understood as resulting from the soul's concern that our daily activities fulfill the soul's mission on earth.

The ideals of the soul, truths it has garnered from countless experiences, are the standard the soul uses in evaluating the experiences of the physical personality. The impressions the soul receives, comparing our daily activities to its storehouse of wisdom in the superconscious mind, are the basis of the dreams we have at night. The soul has an "ah-ha" experience of revelation, but what we remember of that experience is a dream.

We remember few of our dreams and only incomplete portions of those we do recall. The symbolic stories we call dreams are the translations made by the subconscious for the conscious of the soul's experience while we slept. They are an indirect record of what happened. Yet our dreams are perhaps the primary source of clues that we live more than the material life of time and space. For many primitive cultures, dreams were the primary evidence for the reality of the soul.

Dreams are an instructive altered state of consciousness. In our dreams, reality is rubbery. People change identities easily, scenes change instantly. We do impossible things, ridiculous things. We perform miracles and commit horrors. Yet we take this make-believe world to be reality. Dreams prove to us that we ourselves create the sense of reality. The dream is real while we are dreaming it. Only after we awaken do we conclude that we were "only dreaming."

We call some of our dreams "realer than real." We may meet someone special in a dream, perhaps a loved one or someone deceased, and we experience such closeness with that person that upon awakening, we can't believe that it was just a dream. This strange quality of ultrareality makes it easy to accept the evidence for telepathy. Furthermore, dreams that later come true suggest that our dreams are one step ahead of reality.

Cayce emphasized that dreams are real experiences. They are real experiences of the soul. The evaluations the soul makes serve as subconscious guides to our future activities. While we dream, the soul scans ahead to forecast the likely outcome of various attitudes and actions that are competing for our attention. It sorts through various mental patterns and selects new ones to place within the projector to be cast out upon the screen of life. Dreams thus are like seeds of our future experiences. What we call real life is but the consequence of our dreams.

Voluntary Control of Altered States of Consciousness

Sleep and dreams are everyday occurrences of altered states of consciousness. Hidden within them are the secrets of the mind and its creative link with reality. For the most part, we are their passive subjects. We *fall* asleep; we do not drive ourselves to sleep. Dreams *happen* to us; we do not consciously choose to dream, nor what to dream. At least that is the way we experience these two states of mind.

It does not have to be that way. These two activities do not have to remain as involuntary instincts. We can learn to have some conscious control over these and other altered states of consciousness. Being able to enter a desired state of consciousness for a specific purpose is an important part of using the powers of the mind.

We can learn to fall asleep at will. We can approach sleep with a purpose, such as to change our mood, to heal ourselves, or to merge prayerfully with universal awareness. We can learn to cultivate the power of dreams. Dreams are also a means of healing, as well as a source of guidance. We can learn to prepare ourselves to have dreams that provide help with specific problems.

How can we learn to voluntarily enter a special state of consciousness? Learning to go into an altered state of consciousness requires a special approach. It is learning to initiate processes that would ordinarily happen involuntarily. It involves invoking the will through an indirect means. Cayce gave a general principle for learning this type of skill. He called it "setting self aside."

Setting Self Aside

Squeeze your right hand into a fist. As you do so, notice that it requires that you make an effort. Feel the tension along the back of your hand and along your forearm. Squeezing your fist is something that *you do*. It is an active, direct action on your part. The tension you feel in your arm and hand is the experience of what *you are doing*.

Now allow your fist to open, allow your arm to relax. Can you *make* your arm relax? You can try shaking it or rubbing it. Such actions may help your arm relax, but it doesn't *make* it relax. Your arm can only relax itself, as you *allow it*, if you are *willing* to have it relax. Try it again. Make a fist momentarily until you can feel the tension, then release your fist and allow your arm to relax. See if you can set yourself aside, get out of the way, and simply allow your arm to relax itself. It relaxes when you *do nothing*. Relaxing is something your body will do itself when you allow it. It requires nothing from you other than that you allow it to happen and do nothing to interfere with the natural, unfolding process of relaxation.

Learning to voluntarily enter an altered state of consciousness requires learning to set self aside and allow the altered state to happen by itself. Yet it requires that you intend for it to happen, to be willing for it to happen, and then to allow it to happen.

It is learning the secret of a paradox, of a seemingly contradictory maneuver. How do you get out of your own way? How do you pick yourself up and set yourself aside? Who picks up whom and who sets whom aside? Setting self aside in order to enter an altered state of consciousness isn't something you can do in the same active way that you can make a fist. You have to intend it, yet you have to allow it to happen by itself.

The paradox of setting self aside will prove important not only in learning to enter altered states of consciousness but also in learning to use visualization. It is also the key principle in learning how to allow your ideals to guide the development of your life. It is a key to spiritual unfoldment. The secret to this seemingly mysterious yet quite simple principle is discovered within our will. It is the special, active receptivity we have called *willingness*. You set yourself aside, you allow your body to relax, you enter altered states of consciousness and use visualization techniques by your focused willingness to have it happen.

To learn this quality of willingness, we need to turn to another altered state of consciousness. It is the one Cayce would have us become skilled in first. It will help in all the others.

Meditation

Meditation may evoke images of shaven heads, colorful robes, strange postures, exotic chants, and religious cults. Yet meditation is actually something more ordinary than its publicity would suggest, while more profound and important than any publicity statement could ever convey. Cayce stressed it above any other activity, except for the setting of ideals, and it has the support of a substantial body of scientific evidence. We will approach meditation from a starting point that is quite familiar to you.

In the second chapter of this book, I suggested an experiment for you to try. I asked you to see if you were in control of your mind by trying to hold your thoughts to a single focus. Perhaps you might repeat that experiment for a moment to refresh your memory for how it feels to try it and what happens. The result is a convincing demonstration that you can't control your mind. No matter how hard you try to pin your thoughts to a single focus, the spontaneous flow of your mind is stronger than your efforts.

You can't bring enough willpower to bear to keep your mind from wandering. We discussed the problem of will in Chapter Nine. We use our will to make choices. It expresses our individuality. The wanderings of our attention reflect the activity of our will. Our will, however, is not the same as willpower. Willpower alone cannot make our mind stay focused. Until we can learn how to have our mind settle on a single focus, we cannot say that we have gained any mastery of our will.

Meditation is the practice of the will. It is an altered state of consciousness that happens when we intentionally are willing to allow the mind to rest on a single focus. It is the practice of becoming mentally attuned to our ideal. It is the training ground for learning to set self aside. Let's learn to meditate.

How to Meditate

Here is a simple way to begin to meditate. It is as simple as releasing your fist, if you are willing to allow it to be that simple.

Get into a comfortable, upright position in your chair.

Assume a posture that will allow your body to balance itself so that you will not have to make any effort at all to remain in that position. Close your eyes and sense your body. Make any necessary adjustments to your posture to make yourself comfortable.

Keeping your eyes closed, take a deep breath and hold it. When it becomes stressful to hold it any longer, let it go. Notice how good it feels to let your breath go. Meditation can feel that good.

Gently focus on your breathing. It comes and it goes. Notice the feel of your breathing. When it comes, your abdomen expands as your lungs fill with air. There is a slight tension. When the air goes, your body relaxes. The cycle of breathing is irregular. Some breaths are long and some are short. But breathing always happens!

Follow your breathing closely while allowing the breathing to happen by itself. For days, months, and years your breathing has functioned without any assistance from you. Now that you are paying attention to it, that doesn't mean you need to interfere with it. In fact, one of the easiest ways to learn the secret of setting yourself aside is to learn to be able to watch your breath without interfering with it. You may have noticed that as you watched your breathing, you automatically stepped in and began regulating it in some manner. Now step aside and simply observe your breathing without interfering with it. Allow yourself to trust the breathing process. It can be quite comforting.

It's natural for your mind to generate thoughts about your breathing as you observe it. That's OK. Your mind will also naturally wander and think about other things. Your breathing's not *that* interesting. That's OK. When you notice that you are thinking thoughts, think to yourself the thought, "That's OK." Then let your attention return to your breathing, resting in the comforting rhythm of the waves of breath. Your mind will soon wander again, off into its own thoughts. That's OK. Gently return your attention to rest on your breath. Simply practice the willingness to have your attention remain peacefully focused on your breathing. That's meditation.

You may well fall asleep. It's that comforting. Many people reported to Cayce that they fell asleep when they tried to meditate. He indicated that it was perfectly OK to do so. It was a sign that the body needed the rest. It is also a way for the conscious mind, when it is first introduced to meditation, to use sleep to seek reminders from the soul's universal awareness concerning the meaning and purpose of meditation. If you fall asleep when you first practice this meditation, assume you did so to receive reassurance from your soul about the safety and value of meditation.

Add Meaning to Meditation

Meditation is not a meaningless activity. Focusing on the breath is a natural way to place the mind in harmony with the flow of the spirit. It is the breath of life. Another word for inhalation is *inspiration*. Being infused with the spirit, and receiving spiritual or creative insight, share a common word because they share a common process. Allowing yourself to be inspired while you meditate begins with setting self aside and allowing your breath to come to you on its own.

You may wish to explicitly add a mental component to your meditation to reflect your greater awareness of the meaning of meditaton. To do so, think the phrase "I am" as the breath comes in. Think the word *One* as the breath goes out. As you let go, letting your breath go out, as you set self aside, preparing for the moment of receiving inspiration, your thoughts follow a parallel track: "I am . . . One . . . I am . . . One." Physical sensations and mental meaning now coincide. Still, your mind will wander. That's OK. When you find your mind thinking other thoughts, simply return your attention to your breathing and allow your mind to reflect, "I am . . . One . . . I am . . . One." That is meditation.

Echoes in Your Mind

Let's pause for a moment and try another experiment. Take a single word, like *apple*, and say it silently to yourself. As you do so, listen to what it sounds like in your mind as you say it. After you say it once, listen carefully. You can hear the word echo in your mind. See how many repeating echoes you can hear of the word *apple* before it fades away.

What happened? I trust that you could hear the echo. Maybe just a few times, perhaps many times. Perhaps you also noticed the intriguing fact that it became hard to tell if you were hearing an echo or were listening to yourself repeat the word. Listening to the echo has both the qualities of listening to something and thinking something. It is like listening because you have to be receptive. It is like thinking because it is concentrating on a process happening in your mind.

Listening to a word echo in your mind is a way to allow your mind to think the same thought over and over. It's a much easier way than to directly try to force your mind to stay focused on a single thought. Rather than tightening your jaw and forcing your mind to stay focused, you relax and allow yourself to listen to a thought that automatically repeats itself. It repeats itself as long as you are willing to listen to it. When your will takes your attention to other thoughts, all you have to do is think the original word again, and be willing to listen to it repeat itself. Listening to the repeated echo of your own thought is practice in the paradox of setting self aside. It is an indirect approach to a goal that can't be reached directly. It is meditation.

The Ideal of Meditation

Clearly, meditation is not emptying the mind. It is not making the mind go blank. Cayce emphasized that the goal of meditation is *not* a blank mind. The goal is to attune the mind to a single focus. Cayce's approach to meditation is to attune the mind to our chosen ideal. That ideal could be the breath and the idea of oneness with the spirit, if that is your ideal. If love is your ideal, then make love the focus of meditation. Meditation is the willingness to listen to the reverberations of your ideal. It is the discipline, not of making the mind empty of all thoughts, but of choosing to bring the mind back to the ideal every time it strays to other thoughts.

Here is where meditation is a training ground for the will. Here is where we can learn to be willing to choose to entertain only a specific mental pattern and ignore others. During meditation, we practice returning to our ideal, even though other mental patterns compete for our attention. It is where we learn that, rather than using will power, we must be willing to surrender to an ideal. We set self, and all the ideas its will is bringing to our attention, aside, in favor of attuning to our ideal.

An ideal is an image of perfection or ultimate good that cannot be achieved in actual practice. It guides the way, but is never a goal that can be reached. Similarly, in meditation, the goal of having nothing in mind except the thought of the ideal, to have every cell in one's body, all our feelings and thoughts in total harmony with the ideal, is itself only an ideal. It guides the process of meditation, but shouldn't be used as an expectation of what we will always experience. It is something that we can aim for, but it cannot be forced. Yet the process can happen by itself, if you'll simply set self aside.

Fear of Meditation

Since you become more aware of the presence of your subconscious mind during meditation, you may judge that it has become more active. You are aware of a lot of thinking. You may experience thoughts or emotions that disturb you.

Some people believe that meditation is like taking the lid off the subconscious. They feel that it is almost like inviting disturbing thoughts that would normally be held in check to now flood the mind. They experience anxiety during meditation. They find meditation fearful.

It is that mental picture of meditation as opening Pandora's box, and the resulting expectation, that is partly responsible for this effect. Meditation, however, is the practice of allowing yourself to maintain a focus on a positive affirmation while ignoring other thoughts. It is not an invitation to the subconscious to speak up, nor is it required that negative thoughts be stopped.

An interesting laboratory experiment in "thought stopping" may be instructive. Researchers at Trinity University asked subjects to observe their stream of thought for five minutes, but to *not think* of a white bear. Subjects were only fairly successful. Thoughts of white bears managed to creep into the stream of thought. Afterward, they were allowed to think whatever they liked. During that rest period, they found that thoughts of white bears were even more frequent! In other words, not only was it difficult to try *not* to think a particular thought; but also, after stopping this effort, the thought persisted with a vengeance!

The researchers then tried a different tactic with a new

group of subjects. These subjects were also told to not think of a white bear. In case they did, however, they were told to then think of a red Volkswagen instead. These subjects were better able to avoid thinking of a white bear than the first group of subjects who had no alternative focus. Moreover, during their subsequent free-thought period, hardly any thoughts of white bears came to mind.

There is a lesson here. Fighting a thought is next to impossible. If you do fight it, then once you rest your defenses, the thought attacks more ferociously. Don't fight your thoughts. Don't say, "I won't think about that!" Rather, say, "I will choose to think about this instead!" Meditation is not the attempt to stop thinking. It is the practice of choosing to return one's attention back to the ideal when other thoughts come into mind.

What Happens in Meditation

Although you do very little during meditation, a lot happens.

Your body slows down. Breathing becomes more regular, heart rate and blood pressure decrease, and there is a general relaxing effect.

The subconscious mind is also relaxing. It becomes less active and less responsive. Because your body is relaxed, there is less emotional response to the thoughts that arise from within the subconscious. Whereas one thought might normally trigger ten more thoughts, during meditation a thought finds comparatively little response. The subconscious is settling down, even though it may not seem that way to you.

Cayce's description of what happens in meditation emphasizes the activity of the spiritual ideal upon the thoughts, the emotions and the body of the meditator. We can think about an ideal, but when we meditate upon it, it has relatively more power to shape our being. As the body and the subconscious mind relax, the effect of the ideal increases as our imagination is filled with its meaning.

Imagine watching a movie when all the theater lights are on. The picture on the screen is not very bright, and it is easy to be distracted by the sights and sounds within the theater. When the lights go out, the picture on the screen becomes the reality. Similarly, during meditation, the thoughts and bodily reactions that would normally reduce the influence of the ideal are turned down. The patterning power of the ideal then has maximum effect.

Every atom in the body begins to resonate with the ideal during meditation. The activity of the endocrine system begins to reflect the influence of our ideal. The body's immune system, governed by the thymus gland, becomes stronger. This documented and measured effect is evidence of Cayce's statement that meditation on a spiritual ideal improves the harmonious functioning of the psychic centers and their corresponding endocrine glands.

While your ideal is transforming your mental, emotional, and physical being during meditation, you are learning to turn to the will of your higher self. You are learning to substitute a spiritual willingness for personal willpower. You are also learning to enter an altered state of consciousness where you allow a particular pattern of mind to become your reality. You are also, as research has verified, increasing your sensitivity to psychic awareness. The practice of meditation, grounded in absorption in your ideal, will help you learn to master other states of consciousness. It is the gateway to the hidden powers of your mind.

11

Self-Hypnosis and
the Power of Suggestion

*Begin with the study of self, which may be best
done by suggestive forces to the body through
hypnosis.*

Edgar Cayce 3483-1

No doubt you have heard stories of the dramatic power of
hypnosis. Hypnosis has been used to remove warts, stop
bleeding, and eliminate pain.

After undergoing a period of scorn, hypnosis was accepted in 1959 by the American Medical Association as a useful
adjunct to medical analgesia. Hypnosis can be so effective
as a painkiller that it has been used in place of surgical
anesthesia in both cesarian section deliveries and amputations.

These miracles of hypnosis reveal the powers of the
mind. Yet such amazing stories make hypnosis look like
some deeply mysterious and magical potion. It makes hypnosis seem far removed from our ordinary life. One moment
we glimpse the powers of the mind, then they disappear
behind the veil of a secret process.

The truth of the matter is that hypnosis is quite ordinary. We enter states of hypnosis every day. Each night as we fall asleep, we pass through a hypnotic state. We become lost in thought, hypnotized by our daydreams. Our favorite television show absorbs our attention. The story is real to us, and we laugh and cry. We are hypnotized by the electronic reality in front of us. We are subject to the suggestions implicit in television commercials. Our days our filled with the events of hypnosis. Three very ordinary processes are involved in hypnosis: relaxation, suggestion, and imagery. Under the right circumstances, any one of these processes may create a hypnotic effect.

Hypnotic effects occur through the action of the subconscious mind. The subconscious operates through suggestion and imagery. When the conscious mind is relaxed, the subconscious mind can be reached directly. It is thus easiest to work with hypnosis in a special state of relaxation. Hypnosis is simply a way to communicate with the subconscious.

The Presleep State: Self-Hypnosis Every Night

The time of falling asleep at night, Cayce noted, is the most natural hypnotic state. You've experienced hypnosis every night of your life!

As we fall asleep, you may recall, the body relaxes and the senses shut down. The conscious mind dims. As external reality fades away, our own thoughts become reality. The subconscious mind emerges as the dominating consciousness. The subconscious accepts its imaginings as reality.

The time of falling asleep is a perfect time to make suggestions to the subconscious mind. Cayce often recommended the presleep state as a golden opportunity to plant thought seeds of a new life. We will learn how to use the presleep state ourselves, to give our subconscious mind positive programming. It can become a major tool in using deeper mind power to achieve our goals.

Cayce also advised parents to use the presleep state to the child's advantage. It is a natural extension of the bedtime story and bedtime prayers. It is a time to help the child establish a positive outlook on life. It is also a time to plant positive alternatives to problem behaviors.

Cayce prescribed to parents the use of presleep suggestion for children's psychological, psychosomatic, and physical problems as well: nightmares, bedwetting, bad habits, as well as conditions such as hyperactivity. The subconscious mind controls the operation of the body. It stands in between our thoughts and their physical consequences. Thus, Cayce recommended the use of presleep suggestion to shape the influence of the subconscious in bringing healing to the body.

The Miracle of Jennifer

One of the most dramatic cases of the use of suggestion in restoring a child to health is told by a mother, Cynthia Pike Ouellette, in her book *The Miracle of Suggestion: The Story of Jennifer*. Because of her mother's own sudden, severe infection, Jennifer was born eleven weeks prematurely. She weighed only two pounds and was infected herself. The doctors said she had no hope of survival, as she was severely jaundiced, suffered from seizures and hydrocephalus, and was experiencing occasional cardiac arrest and difficulty in breathing. Jennifer's mother, however, had reasons to believe that her baby daughter would survive. The next day Jennifer almost died and was saved through a blood transfusion. The doctors were now predicting that *if* Jennifer survived, she would be severely handicapped, with damage to her eyes, brain, and lungs, and would very likely be mentally retarded.

Almost every day in the Newborn Intensive Care Unit, Jennifer suffered some type of setback. Almost every day the doctors discovered another malady in Jennifer's tiny body. Cynthia's faith in her daughter's recovery was unshakable, and she found herself constantly talking to her. She couldn't touch her, as Jennifer's body found touch painful, so mother's only way to be in contact with Jennifer was through talking. She reassured Jennifer that everything would be fine. Then she began to describe for Jennifer how her body was healing itself. Without knowing it at the time, she was giving her daughter suggestions of healing.

By one month, Jennifer weighed three pounds. She was able to leave the intensive-care unit and move into an observational unit. By nine weeks, weighing about six pounds, Jennifer left the hospital to go home with her mother. The problems were not left behind, however, and there were further discouragements. By the seventh month, the doctors' prediction that Jennifer would develop cerebral palsy was confirmed. In a moment of despair, when Jennifer's mother was wondering how her daughter was managing to survive all these problems, it occurred to her that it was because of all their talks. She was convinced of it, and began to research the power of suggestion. It was at that point that she discovered the work of Edgar Cayce and his advice concerning presleep suggestion with children.

What had begun as an instinctive expression of positive suggestions to Jennifer now became a consciously planned and intentionally programmed set of regular suggestion sessions with Jennifer. "You are a perfectly normal creation," she said to Jennifer in a natural tone of voice.

"You are perfect, whole and healthy. Your spine is per-

fect, whole and healthy. . . . You have perfect control of
both hands. . . . You are capable of doing anything you want
to do. . . . You wake up feeling very good every day.'' These
statements are a small sampling of the positive thoughts
Jennifer's mother repeated to her over and again. She also
made tape recordings of these suggestions to play for Jennifer
on a regular basis.

It may seem strange to expect such verbal suggestions,
delivered to a tiny infant, to have any effect on the body.
Can the small baby understand such words? Does the baby's
subconscious mind understand? Cayce indicated that the
subconscious does understand, that mother and infant are
bonded at the subconscious level and that these communica-
tions would be acted upon.

Jennifer's mother also had to train herself to consistently
think in a positive manner. If a visitor asked, ''What is
wrong with Jennifer?'' mother learned to say that nothing
was wrong, that Jennifer was perfectly healthy, and to
believe it.

Against terrible odds, having only the will to live, the
atmosphere of positive suggestions, along with the massages
and other forms of tender loving care, Jennifer gradually
evolved into a healthy young girl.

Subliminal Suggestion and Self-Help Tapes

Positive thinking and autosuggestion has been a popular
self-help strategy since the early 1900s. Today it has taken
on more sophistication. Prerecorded audiocassettes containing self-help suggestions have become a mass-market
item. Especially appealing are the tapes that offer subliminal suggestions hidden within pleasant background
music.

Stick a portable cassette player in your pocket. Place a

tiny earphone discreetly in your ear. As you go about your business, at work and at home, you hear soothing music. All the while, you realize, subliminal messages are silently nudging your subconscious. You are free from smoke, you are thin, you are healthy, wealthy, and wise. As you pursue your normal routine, your subconscious mind is imprinting a new program for living. It requires no effort on your part. You simply reap the benefits of the principles of dynamic psychology applied with the latest in modern technolgoy.

It sounds too good to be true. Although based on sound and established principles, subliminal tapes promise more than they deliver. Cayce would suggest, on the other hand, that they deliver something that they don't mention. The issue of commercial tapes, offering suggestions and subliminal suggestions, deserves some detailed discussion.

It is true that the subconscious mind is capable of detecting information that is invisible to the conscious mind. It is quite sensitive to subliminal stimulation. We have already examined some of the research that indicates the incredible extent of this sensitivity. Subliminal stimulation definitely is a way to bypass the conscious mind and communicate directly with the subconscious. That much is true.

One problem, however, is that subliminal stimulation is a fickle process. For example, to place a voice script into some music so that the voice functions as a subliminal message requires experimental testing to get it right. If the voice is too loud, anyone can hear the message. It's no longer subliminal. If the voice is too soft, only the most discriminating subconscious mind detects it. Many others miss it. The conditions under which the recording is then listened to will also influence whether or not the subliminal message will get through.

Laboratory research on subliminal stimulation requires extensive pretesting to find the exact intensity needed to create the subliminal effect for the average listener. Because any melody will vary in loudness from moment to moment, the laboratory must calibrate each insertion to fit with the loudness of that part of the music. These seemingly minor technical considerations are very important. They are also time-consuming and can be expensive.

Assuming that a commercial producer of subliminal tapes performs the necessary experimentation to properly calibrate the subliminal message, another question then arises. What is the effect on the listener of the subliminal message? As of this writing (spring, 1988), no commercial producer of self-help subliminal-suggestion cassettes has published any studies to indicate that their product does indeed produce changes in people's behavior.

Laboratory research has established that subliminal stimulation affects how a person experiences the foreground stimulation. If I show you a picture of a person's face, for example, I can use subliminal stimulation to affect how you will interpret the expression on that face. If I subliminally flash the word *angry*, superimposing it over the face, you will interpret the person's expression as being more angry than if I flash the word *happy*. Earlier we saw how subliminal messages hidden in a piece of music affected the listener's daydream and associations to the music. In other words, what researchers have learned most about subliminal stimulation is how it influences conscious experience. It tends to bend our conscious perceptions in a direction suggested by the subliminal message. That fact is quite well established.

Contrary to popular opinion, however, most of the research on subliminal stimulation has *not* focused on motivational suggestion. It is commonly assumed that research on subliminal stimulation has studied the effect of messages like "Buy popcorn!" on people's popcorn-buying habits. There have been very few published studies, actually, of that sort, and they have yielded contradictory results.

The popular imagination may assume that Big Brother has been working hard in secret laboratories learning how to influence people through subliminal suggestion. Big Brother, however, has not published the results of this research.

Mommy and I Are One

However, there has been a substantial body of published research investigating the positive effects on behavior of one particular subliminal suggestion. To be effective, it requires a situation where a person is *already motivated* toward a particular goal and is *already making active efforts* to reach that goal. In such cases, exposure to this subliminal message has proven to substantially improve a person's success. Mathematics students scored higher on their math quizzes. People in therapy for depression experienced an elevation of their mood. People in treatment for drug addiction, alcoholism, or smoking were able to abstain for much longer periods of time. These are just the sorts of subliminal-suggestion effects we would desire.

What was the suggestion? It will surprise you. It's not the sort of suggestion you would think to give to yourself. In fact, Lloyd H. Silverman, Ph.D., the psychologist who invented the suggestion, has indicated that the suggestion works only because the conscious mind is *not* aware of its contents. The suggestion is, "Mommy and I are one."

Arguing from a psychoanalytic point of view, Dr. Silverman explains that the suggestion activates an unconscious fantasy of returning to the womb. It is a fantasy that most of us would not consciously find appealing. Planted as a seed thought in the subconscious mind, however, it inspires visions of blissful union with Mom. The visible result is an

overall positive one. There is evidence of increased relaxation, improved mood, decreased dependency upon drugs,
and improved competitive performance. You couldn't ask
for more.

A commercial firm advertising a "Mommy and I are
one" subliminal tape could promise, with some validity,
that listening to its product will produce profound effects.
No such tape is available commercially. It's uncertain whether
or not such a theme would have public appeal. It doesn't
have the ring of success.

In his book *The Search for Oneness*, Dr. Silverman
states, "Unconscious oneness fantasies can enhance adapta-
tion if, simultaneously, a sense of self can be preserved." It
is interesting that, even though coming from a different
point of view, Edgar Cayce made a similar proposal. On
many occasions his psychic source said that the purpose of
each human life is to realize oneness with God *while
simultaneously* developing one's true individuality. The conscious mind, as we have explained, has difficulty understanding and accepting this seemingly paradoxical statement. Presented as a subliminal suggestion, however, it
bypasses the conscious mind to find an exuberant reception
in the subconscious.

I find an important lesson in Silverman's research. By
using subliminal stimulation, motivational suggestions can
be given to the subconscious mind in a way that totally
bypasses the desires of the conscious mind. These suggestions, however, must appeal to the mentality of the subconscious mind. When they do, the subconscious has a strong
response. The response cannot always be predicted. Psychoanalytic reasoning, based upon the peculiar logic of the
subconscious, is necessary to adequately steer the suggestion process. Thus, when we use subliminal tapes we are
dependent upon the insights and wisdom of the manufactur-

er in their choice of suggestions. Even then, we are not certain of the outcome.

Side Effects of Subliminal Suggestion Tapes

Cayce's readings on the possibilities of influence through the subconscious mind suggest another reason to avoid subliminal tapes until such time as they might be made in a different fashion. When we listen to a subliminal tape, we are giving permission to our subconscious mind to be influenced by outside stimulation. Cayce indicates that the influence is not limited to the actual verbal message that might be subliminally embedded on the tape. The influence goes much further than that. The thoughts, feelings, and subconscious motivations of everyone involved in the manufacture of the tape is a potential source of subliminal influence upon the listener!

A similar situation may exist in the reaction the postal-delivery person receives from many dogs. Dog bites are the most serious and frequent occupational hazard of the postal delivery system. Our dog barks and threatens to attack most every person who approaches our house, but he saves his most menacing welcome for the postal worker, regardless of who that might be. No salesperson or UPS delivery person receives the kind of treatment that the postal worker has to endure. I've asked around for some explanation to this phenomenon. The most convincing explanation that I uncovered was that the problem was the bag of mail. A couple of hundred letters, each one handled by several different people, created a very confusing sachet. The postal worker arrives with an ambiguous and mixed message bombarding the dog's nose.

Our subconscious mind can be as sensitive to the emotional vibrations of others as a dog is to scents. When we

open ourselves to influence by listening to a tape containing suggestions, subliminal or otherwise, we can pick up
the emotions and thoughts not only of the person who
voiced the suggestions, but also from the people who
handled your particular copy of the tape when it was
manufactured.

Those experienced in hypnosis will verify that a hypnotic
subject often picks up on the thoughts of the hypnotist. I
once experienced a dramatic example of this phenomenon. I
was attending a hypnosis workshop and was entering a
hypnotic trance following the suggestions of the hypnotist.
As I became more relaxed and his voice became my only
thought, I suddenly had a brief dream. I was in a room that
was totally empty. I noticed that one wall was developing a
hole in it close to the floor. It was as if the wall were a
curtain and someone was lifting the curtain at one spot.
Then a person came through that hole and entered the room.
I found that curious, but then returned to listening to the
hypnotist's voice. As I listened, however, I was startled to
discover that there was now a difference in how I was
experiencing the voice. I was having my own thoughts, and
I was thinking the suggestions myself before the voice
spoke them. It was hard to believe, but as I allowed it to
continue, I was able to verify that I was indeed thinking the
suggestions, word for word, before I heard them.

Afterward, I discussed this experience with the hypnotist.
He explained that what I had experienced was telepathy, that
we had entered into a mind lock together. I reflected on my
dream. A room can represent a state of mind. Under the
relaxed, hypnotic state, my mind was empty. The wall, or
mental barrier, was flexible, like a curtain. The hypnotist
had penetrated that wall and had entered my mind. He told
me that I should remember that experience when I used
hypnosis when working with others. The subject will be

influenced not only by the suggestions that you verbalize, but also by your silent thoughts.

In giving instructions on the preparation of healing materials and devices, Cayce indicated that it was necessary for those involved to first purify themselves with meditation and prayers prior to starting each work session. Those handling the physical materials as well, such as the blank tapes, the copying machine, and the packaging of the tapes, should also be involved in these purification practices. Until such time as manufacturers produce tapes in such a manner, it would be better if we made our own suggestion tapes, or with the help of a like-minded person.

Cayce's instructions about the manufacture of healing aids are no different from what was traditionally practiced by spiritual healers among so-called primitive groups. Native Americans, for example, would dip their healing objects in sacred smoke to purify their vibrations. Such practices seem strange to someone who doesn't appreciate the power of the subconscious mind to be influenced by the thoughts of others. Evidence for psychometry, the ability to read someone's thoughts by holding an object that person has touched, further supports the wisdom of Cayce's advice.

To appreciate how open you are when you avail yourself of a subliminal-suggestion tape, you might try observing your responses to listening to such a tape. My first exposure to such a tape was with one offering suggestions to quit smoking. Playing in the foreground was the sound of the ocean. It was quite a pleasant listening experience. I couldn't hear, of course, what subliminal suggestions I was receiving. But I found that I was constantly thinking about what they might be, wondering what my subconscious was hearing. Not knowing what the facts were, I found that my imagination went wild, supposing all sorts of suggestions. I also found that any resistances I had to the idea of quitting smoking were revealing themselves to me. I felt my ability to smoke was being drained away from me involuntarily, and I was not necessarily willing to have that happen. I would smoke during the tape and would also feel guilty about doing so. Was I defeating the purpose of the suggestions, or was their subliminal power so strong that they would overtake my willful continuation of smoking? I realized that even if there were no suggestions on the tape at all, I was submitting myself to a potent placebo treatment. The very idea that you are listening to a tape containing subliminal suggestions is a very suggestive experience in itself! I found that one clear value of listening to a subliminal-suggestion tape was discovering, by monitoring my thoughts, whether or not I was actually willing to have the suggestions take effect.

Suggestion and Pretending

In the second chapter, we noted that Cayce emphasized that we respect the subconscious mind. He noted its special qualities. In particular, he noted that, in contrast to the conscious mind, the subconscious responds to suggestion. Let's examine what that statement means.

Let me suggest to you, for example, that this book is as light as a feather.

What happened?

You probably checked the weight of the book, feeling it in your hands and noting its weight. In other words, you automatically attempted to evaluate my suggestion. The response of the conscious mind to a statement is to immediately evaluate it. It attempts a verification. The conscious mind tests the statement for truth or accuracy.

Unless it chooses to ignore a statement, or doesn't understand it, the conscious mind automatically tends to agree or disagree with it. It checks it for logic, for consistency with past experience, or with information from its senses, and then either denies or affirms the statement. The conscious mind cannot accept suggestion. As Cayce pointed out, the conscious mind can only respond to a statement as a proposition. It must evaluate the statement, and either validate or deny it.

Let me now instead ask that you *pretend* that your book is as light as a feather. Pretend that the book is so light that you can relax your hands and arms and the book will simply rest in your hands, suspended by itself. Try that and see what happens.

If you pretended, could you experience the book as light? If you did, then try it again, and notice how you go about pretending that the book is light.

How did you do it? You probably focused on certain things and purposefully ignored others. To pretend that the book is as light as a feather, you might focus on how relaxed your hands and arms feel. You might notice the book sitting in your hands, but ignore any sensation of pressure from the book sitting upon your hands. You could then imagine the book sitting weightlessly in your hands.

While pretending, your conscious mind doesn't respond to the statement as a proposition. Instead, it agrees to accept the statement as true and acts accordingly. It focuses its attention on aspects of its experience that would be consistent with that assumption. It ignores contrary data.

Pretending is the best way to explain to the conscious mind what is meant by a suggestion. Otherwise, the conscious mind has no way to respond to a suggestion other than taking it as a proposition.

Recall, from our earlier discussion about attitude change, that we presented Cayce's idea that behaving *as if* you were experiencing a certain attitude, that attitude would come about. We are seeing this principle once again, this time as we see how pretending is a way for the conscious mind to cooperate with the power of suggestion. We can see now how Cayce's advice that we take actions consistent with an attitude we would like to adopt is actually based on an · understanding of how suggestion operates.

All Suggestions Are Affirmations

There is nothing about a statement itself that qualifies it as a suggestion. A statement becomes a suggestion when it is accepted, when it is acted upon, when a person is willing to pretend that it is so, or believe that it is so.

The subconscious mind automatically accepts statements as affirmations of what is true. This characteristic of the subconscious, however, comes with a particular proviso. The subconscious mind does not understand the meaning of the negative *no*, or *not*. If you are given the suggestion, "You will *not* think about the eye of a camel," the subconscious mind drops the word *not* from what it hears. The phrase "eye of the camel" is implanted in the subconscious, and you can't help but think about it. Recalling the experiment in thought stopping we described in the last chapter, we realize it would be more effective to suggest instead, "If you think of the eye of a camel, you will immediately begin thinking about a red Volkswagen."

Understanding of the logic of the negative *not* is the sole province of the conscious mind. In Chapter Three, I described how the creation of the conscious mind arose from an act of negation, separating itself from the subconscious by saying "No." It was likened to a child going through the terrible twos who separates from the parents and establishes its own will by defying the parental will with a constant "No." It is another reason why statements made to the subconscious mind become suggestions, whereas the same statements made to the conscious mind are taken as propositions. The conscious mind always has a "No" ready, and will be quick to use it if the statement doesn't ring true.

The subconscious mind cannot be directed away from an undesirable focus by asking it *not* to do this or that. Instead it must be *re*directed, by asking it to do, or to look at, something else. Here again we have the general Cayce principle of supplanting negatives with positives. Suggestions must be phrased in an affirmative manner. What is it you want the subconscious to believe, to do, to experience?

I have witnessed the use of suggestion to redirect the smoking habit, for example, into other avenues of expression. In one case, this suggestion was gradually established: "When you have the urge to smoke a cigarette, you will experience the taste and smell of vomit and you will reach for your polished stone and feel peaceful while holding it." In another case, the suggestion was based on a spiritual ideal: "When you feel the need to smoke, you will take a deep breath and feel grateful and at peace as the Spirit of God enters you, filling you with love and warmth. You will sigh a deep sigh of relief that the Comforter is so close at hand."

In both cases, there was real motivation to stop smoking, reinforced by their doctors' warnings concerning imminent health dangers. There was also a sincere willingness to quit. Both people had quit smoking except for two or three times a day during moments of stress. At those moments, they couldn't get the mind off having a cigarette. The use of these suggestions planted a different thought habit for those moments. The suggestions didn't have to create a willingness in these people, only a new route through which to express that willingness. In each case, the suggestion was phrased in terms of creating an alternative habit.

A good place to begin learning about how the power of suggestion works through affirmation is with your statement of an ideal. Try wording your statement so that it reads as an affirmation of a fact—not a wish, or a desire, but a fact. Rather than "I want to be a loving person," affirm "I am a person created by love and expressing love." An alternative might be, "Only love is real."

Working with suggestion does not mean pounding the thought into your mind in an attempt to drive out other thoughts. A suggestion, as an affirmation of truth, is expressed in a casual, matter-of-fact manner, in a normal tone of voice, as if to imply, "Of course, no doubt about it." If you announce your affirmation to yourself, shouting it in your mind, as it were, you challenge your conscious mind to take it as a proposition to evaluate. You invite negative reactions.

Repeat your ideal to yourself gently from time to time, willing to pretend it *is* true, willing to believe it as fact. Let yourself *feel* it in your body, let your imagination play with the implications of the affirmation. Let it grow on you. In this way, you will discover for yourself how suggestions operate through affirmation.

Pretending Your Way Into Hypnosis

One of the major difficulties in learning self-hypnosis is not fear of the unknown, but the habit of the conscious mind to evaluate. It's hard not to ask yourself, "Am I really hypnotized now?" You can learn to hynotize yourself more easily if you are willing to pretend that you are hypnotized.

Choosing to pretend that a proposition is true is not the same as evaluating it and deciding it is true. It means to accept the statement as true and direct attention in such a way as to help make the proposition appear true. The conscious mind pretends by focusing on what is consistent with the proposition and ignoring any contradictory information.

Pretending is a good equivalent of suggestion. When the conscious mind becomes so active in its pretending that it forgets that it is pretending, when it begins to now believe what it was pretending to be true, it has come the closest it can to accepting a suggestion.

Entering hypnosis is simply the process of accepting one suggestion after another. Hypnosis is the state of mind of accepting suggestions. As in other suggestions, the conscious mind can help the process of entering hypnosis by the use of pretending.

Researchers have found that instructing people to pretend that they are hypnotized can produce as good hypnotic results as does actual hypnosis. Some argue that this fact shows that there is no such thing as hypnosis. Don't be fooled by this argument. When the conscious mind pretends, it is performing the conscious equivalent of what the subconscious mind does when it accepts a suggestion.

The conscious mind can cooperate with what the subconscious mind is doing. If the conscious mind is still active under hypnosis, it will experience its response to suggestions as pretending. That doesn't invalidate the experience. It only helps.

Traditional hypnosis theory maintains that people vary in their ability to be hypnotized. Cayce maintained that anyone could learn how to enter a hypnotic state simply because it is a natural state of consciousness. Modern thinking about hypnosis is changing in favor of Cayce's point of view. Research has now demonstrated that the conscious mind can cooperate with the induction of hynotic suggestions by agreeing to pretend. By being willing to imagine the suggestions, the conscious mind can pave the way for the subconscious to accept suggestions.

The ability to pretend, to imagine or act, initiated by the willingness of the conscious mind, is good for hypnosis. Learning how to become absorbed in an imaginative activity, in fact, is a close equivalent to hypnosis. As we will now discover, a willingness to pretend or imagine can be used as a method of entry to the more traditional hypnotic state of deep relaxation.

Deep Relaxation

Learning to relax is the first step in learning self-hypnosis. The vitality of the conscious mind depends upon the activity of the body and the alertness of the senses. If the body relaxes and we ignore information from our senses, the conscious mind loses the stimulation it depends upon and it begins to evaporate. This is what happens as we begin to fall asleep and it is what happens when entering hypnosis.

There are a number of ways to begin to learn deep relaxation. None requires *doing* anything. Relaxing is the opposite of doing. It is a process of letting go. Relaxation is another example of "setting self aside."

To relax, it is best to either lie down or sit in an easy chair that leans back. Having a pillow under your knees and ankles, as well as under your neck, helps support those areas of the body and adds to your comfort.

An excellent way to begin is with the eyelid method described by Henry Bolduc in *Self-hypnosis*. Cast your gaze upon a spot across the room and close your eyelids slowly, as slowly as you can. Then slowly open them and close them once again, very slowly. Repeat this process ten times. By the tenth time, the area around your eyes will feel very tired and relaxed. The sensation of relaxation can then spread to the rest of your body.

You can focus on the breath and imagine the whole body breathing. Relaxation naturally occurs in the chest and abdomen during every exhalation. Begin by focusing in that region of the body and then moving out to other areas. With each exhalation, for example, pretend that your knees are also exhaling breath. Imagine your knees relaxing as they exhale tension along with the air. Continue this process as you move along to every part of your body.

Some people enjoy saying to themselves "Re-" as they inhale, and "-lax" as they exhale. It provides a mental focus. It also helps to prevent falling asleep until such time as sleep may be the goal.

Another approach to relaxation is to focus on one limb at a time and imagine it as feeling heavy. The sensation of heaviness is what happens when a limb relaxes. It doesn't feel like a lead weight is bearing down on it with pressure. Instead, it feels heavy, as if it were made of lead itself and were melting. It feels very good to let it go and allow it to relax. Here is a way to relax that is based on suggestion and that automatically introduces you to a self-hypnotic state.

Begin by experiencing your right arm as heavy. Say to yourself, "My right arm is heavy." Don't do anything to make it heavy. Simply imagine it as heavy, and be willing to experience it that way. Why don't you try that right now?

Put down this book. Rest your arm on your lap or on the arm of the chair. Close your eyes and let yourself imagine that your arm feels heavy. Pretend that it is heavy by noticing any sensations in your arm that feel like heaviness. Let those sensations spread through your entire arm. After you've enjoyed the experience for a moment, wiggle your fingers and the heaviness will go away.

Wasn't that easy? It's a very natural experience. It's also one of the most common suggestions a hypnotist gives when first beginning a hypnotic induction. You can easily do it yourself.

To go further with this procedure, don't stop at the right arm. After a minute or so, move your attention to your other arm, thinking "My left arm is heavy." Then move along to each of your legs. You can go back and summarize your experience with suggestions such as, "My arms are heavy," "My legs are heavy," or "My arms and legs are heavy."

By imagining your body as relaxed, then experiencing relaxation, you've successfully responded to suggestion. You are on your way to even deeper levels of hypnosis. By imagining your arm as feeling heavy, you have begun, without realizing it, to use imagery in your autosuggestions. As we now turn to the topic of imagery, remember this experience. You do have imagery, and you can use it to control your state of consciousness and your body.

12

The Mind's Eye:
Imagination and Visualization

*Physical conditions—whether pertaining to social,
to money, to station in life, to likes and dislikes—
are the application of those mental images builded
within the body, seated, guided, directed, by the
spiritual. . . .*

Edgar Cayce 349-4

As the eyes are the window to the soul, so is the mind's eye
the window to the soul of the mind. The mind's eye sees
with images and it conceives with images. Nowhere is the
creative magic of the mind more evident than in imagery.

We value people with "vision." It is not their eyesight
we applaud, but their imagination, their ability to see what
is not yet before their eyes. Such people trust those images
in their minds and steer by them, creating actual realities
from what was first only imagined.

Beethoven composed his best symphonies after he had
gone deaf. All he had was his imagination to invent and
polish his music. He never heard it played. Einstein developed

his theory of relativity by first imagining what it would be like to ride upon a ray of light. Much of his theorizing was based upon imaginary experiments. It wasn't until after his death that scientists were even capable of making the actual observations he imagined. Out of his imagination, Walt Disney created a cast of characters and the means to bring them to life. He not only invented an entire reality, but the means to create it in actual physical terms.

Such pioneers, and there have been many, provide proof positive of the saying "What the mind can conceive and believe, the person can achieve."

Cayce would have us know that each of us is a similar pioneer. Each of us is using the powers of what he called the "imaginative forces" of the mind to create our life experiences. Whether or not we are conscious of the process, or are actively engaged in making intentional choices about its use, each of us is drawing upon the creative forces through the imagination to conceive possibilities, to believe in certain eventualities, and to manifest circumstances in the body of our lives. Cayce would have us become more conscious of this process, choose our ideal, and work with the imagination in a more deliberate and constructive fashion.

To do so, we must first recognize that our bias is to think of the imagination as relating to the imaginary, as distinct from the real. We often use the word *imaginary* to mean something that is not real. Instead, if we would lean toward the implications we grant to the term *visionary*, we will be off to a better start in appreciating what Cayce meant by the imaginative forces.

The Intuitive Radar of the Imagination

Your visionary mind is like a television set. It is capable of tuning in to vibrational patterns from around the world and translating them into pictures upon its screen. In fact, it is through the image-making capabilities of the mind that intuitive, psychic, and creative experiences are manifested. The imagination is a mode of experience, of sensing, of picking up information.

Dreams are the place where most of us become aware of the sensitivity of the imagination. While dreaming, our imagination faithfully captures any intuitions or psychic impressions sensed through the soul's infinite reach of perception. We may dream prophetically about an event that later comes true. We may dream telepathically about the troubles of a distant friend. We may reach out clairvoyantly to locate the existence of something that we need. We may dream intuitively the solution to a problem. In our dreams, we may peer into our body with microscopic precision to diagnose the source of a pain. In each case, the dream state uses the imagination to translate impressions into informative, if not also symbolically expressed, visual imagery.

Sometimes it is through feelings that the imagination receives its first intuitive signal. Contemplating these feelings will lead to their translation into images that can then be more easily read for informative meaning. It is like turning the television to a channel that gives some indication of sound, suggesting the presence of a station broadcast, then fine-tuning the television to bring in the picture as well as possible.

For example, consider what happened to a friend of mine, Jane, who confided to her husband, Edward, that she had an uneasy feeling about his boss, Mr. Jones. She was referring to the dinner they had shared with Mr. and Mrs. Jones, where there had been much discussion about the business and Edward's role in developing the company. Edward, enamored with the prospects for the future he was envisioning as a result of that dinner conversation, was reluctant to pay much attention to his wife's vague feelings.

Partly because her husband didn't encourage her to vent these feelings, and partly because his reaction showed her that he wasn't taking seriously her implied warning, Jane found herself reviewing the feeling over and over in her mind. She knew she had to find a way to express herself in a manner that would make her husband sit up and take notice to the threat she just *knew* existed. Focusing on the gut feeling, she experienced various images appearing in her mind. In her imagination, she saw Mr. Jones pulling a rug out from under Edward, and she saw the surprised look on Edward's face as he began to fall. Edward's look of being betrayed, though, didn't quite match her own gut feeling, and she looked again at her image of Mr. Jones. She didn't sense Mr. Jones as intending to harm Edward, but saw him juggling several balls in the air. One ball started to get away from him, and as he chased after it, he inadvertently pulled the rug with him, causing her husband to fall over. Had the rug been nailed down, or not attached to Mr. Jones, his response to this runaway ball wouldn't have affected her husband in the same way. This imaginary scene gave Jane the information she needed.

Jane now approached her husband in a different manner, directing his attention in a more specific direction. She asked him if it was possible that, if Mr. Jones followed up on certain growth directions that might prove promising, company resources would be drained away from the growth projects Edward was going to direct. Edward had to agree that it was a possibility. Jane suggested that Mr. Jones, without intending to, might thus undermine Edward's efforts. He did have a tendency to suddenly grab on to something that was hot, forgetting about previous commitments. Wouldn't it be a good idea, she wondered, for Edward to get some kind of specific contract from Mr. Jones concerning the resources to be committed to Edward's projects? It hadn't occurred to Edward to doubt Mr. Jones's planning, but the more he thought about Jane's insight, the more he suspected she was right.

A few days later, Edward revealed to Jane that he had had some further discussions with Mr. Jones. They had clarified their plans, and in so doing, Edward realized that without Jane's insight, he might have inadvertently accepted an untenable assignment. Edward expressed his gratitude to Jane, who felt relief that her husband's position was now more secure. She herself was grateful that she had spent the time with her feelings, coaching them to reveal what they had to say in such informative imagery.

Jane's story is a good example of how the imagination can tune in to an impression and clarify it by way of mental imagery. Jane trusted her intuition, although she did not understand the meaning of her initial feeling of unease, and allowed her imagination to speak to her more clearly. She was not "imagining things," in the cliché meaning of the phrase, but was instead using her imagination as a channel of ever-clearer intuition.

In our exploration of the subconscious mind in Chapter Two, we saw how its powers of subliminal ESP and creativity operated through the intuitive mode of imagery. We can learn how to intentionally tune in to this level of consciousness and use the intuitive, creative, and psychic skills of the imagination. Our preliminary work, in the previous chapter, learning how to relax ourselves and enter a self-hypnotic state, prepares us for this capability. We are already well on our way.

The Formula for Inspiration: Hypnosis Plus Daydream

John was a free-lance writer. He had been researching an article on a local cooperatively run store. He had gathered all the necessary facts and had written a few paragraphs, but he hadn't been able to come up with an approach to the story that had quite the emotional punch he wanted. John tried hypnosis.

John relaxed in an easy chair. He listened to music, while at the same time listening to instructions designed to take him into a hypnotic state of consciousness. Fifteen minutes later, when the music was over, John listened to further instructions, suggesting he visualize his problem. "Picture in your mind's eye," it was suggested, "all the elements of your magazine article."

John saw three piles of papers. One pile was neatly stacked and was full of writing. It was the completed article. The second pile was quite large, but loosely stacked, papers lying every which way. It was full of little bits and pieces of writing. He saw that all these bits and pieces were the elements of his research, quotations from people in the store, descriptions of the premises, some trial sentences and paragraphs. The third pile was much smaller and was in the dark. There wasn't much in those papers yet, and they troubled John.

John then received a second set of instructions. "Let the images disappear from your mind," it was suggested, "and forget about your problem." John sighed, for he was happy to relax and relieve himself of the burden of thinking about his article. He then heard this suggestion:

"Even though you cannot see these elements any longer, they are still very alive in the back of your mind, out of sight. In fact, they have a life of their own where you can't see them, and in a moment they will cause a dream or dreamlike experience to come into your mind's eye."

Moments later, John was daydreaming about floating in the air down Main Street. He floated right into the second-story window of the store he had been writing about. Once inside the store he continued floating about, viewing the premises from the air. He saw the various departments, the sales personnel, and the customers. He felt the store's atmosphere, and everything within the store took on a special quality. The merchandise vibrated on the shelves, sparkling with light, inviting the customers, "Take me home, I'm good!" He experienced the special feeling that existed between the sales personnel and the customers, who both had a cooperative interest in the store and its success. John found himself feeling very good being in such an atmosphere.

When John woke up from this dream, he was very enthusiastic about writing his magazine article. Within a few minutes he was busy at work, writing the story of a visit to the store. Within an hour, he had completed a rough draft of the entire article. He liked the tone of the article. It had never occurred to him to simply describe the store from the point of view of someone who comes in to visit and browse. He had been bogged down by the technicalities and had missed the spirit of the place. Within a week of leisurely work, he revised his draft, submitted his article, and it was published.

John's story is taken from one of the cases reported by Robert Davé, a psychologist at Michigan State University who studied the usefulness of hypnotic daydreams in creative problem-solving. In his experiment, he invited people who were stuck on a problem to try one of two approaches. The first approach was the hypnotic daydream method John experienced. The second method was to try a rational approach, thinking about the problem without allowing any irrational feelings to interfere with the problem-solving efforts.

People who experienced the rational method received coaching on how to stay focused while they logically thought through each element of their problem. They explained

aloud their problem in detail and went over every possible
element of a solution. Spending up to an hour with their
coach, they examined every relevant idea for its rationality
and appropriateness. At the end of this session, the person
felt quite enthusiastic and expressed the opinion that the
process had been quite helpful.

One week after this experiment, all participants reported
on the status of their problem. The results were dramatic.
Six out of the eight people who had experienced the hypnotic-
daydream method had since worked out a successful solution to their problem. Of the eight people who had engaged
in rational problem-solving, however, only one person had
so far arrived at a satisfactory solution. Even though all the
people who had the rational treatment had thought it beneficial, while only a few of the people experiencing hypnosis
felt that way, the hypnotic daydream had certainly proven to
be the more effective formula for inspiration!

You can learn from John's experience in this research
project. You can use this method to obtain inspirations of
your own. Using the method of self-hypnosis described in
the last chapter, you can enter a relaxed state of mind. You
can then allow your imagination to bring you inspirations on
whatever you suggest.

The philosophy in the Cayce readings would recommend
that you begin work with hypnotic daydreams by focusing
on your ideal. Learn how to have daydreams that portray the
spirit of your ideal in pictures and scenes you can feel. Once
you are relaxed and ready for suggestions, mentally repeat
to yourself your ideal and allow it to create in you the
feelings that it suggests. Then allow those feelings to develop into images. Let yourself have a daydream based on your
ideal.

The next step would be to use the hypnotic daydream
experience to help you imagine how an ideal attitude might
help you respond differently to a particular situation. In your

hypnotic state, allow yourself to get into the feeling of your ideal and then view your current situation. Have a daydream about this situation as you approach it in the mood of your ideal. Very likely, you will find that in your daydream you find a novel way of approaching the situation.

Cayce indicates that the imaginative forces operate within patterns set by an ideal. If you wish to ensure that your use of the inspiration formula yields constructive results, it is important to first develop familiarity with having daydreams centered about the theme of your ideal. As you practice these daydreams, you will likely evolve one or two imaginary scenes that immediately place you in the mood and frame of mind of your ideal. It may be an image of yourself surrounded by light, or sitting in the sun at the beach, or looking out at the world from a mountaintop, or cuddled in the arms of a loving giant. Whatever it may be, you will have developed an image of inspiration. It is just this sort of image that hypnotists often suggest when guiding a hypnotic induction on creative problem-solving. You will have evolved your own imaginary scene and you will find it a very powerful tool for further work with the use of imagination for inspiration and problem-solving.

Presleep Imagery for Seeding Dreams

Using the inspiration formula as you fall asleep at night is a wonderful way to increase the creative power of this technique. It will plant a suggestive seed within your subconscious that will very likely sprout into a full-fledged dream for you to ponder in the morning. The use of dreams for creative inspiration is a powerful approach that invites the participation of the full scope of the superconscious mind to help you in your endeavors.

There is no question, no problem, Cayce indicated, that

can't be solved or answered by asking our dreams for help. He indicated that for personal problems, scientific and religious questions, whatever the topic, the superconscious mind was available in the dream state for guidance and wisdom.

History bears proof of Cayce's claim. In *Our Dreaming Mind: History and Psychology*, Bob Van de Castle, Professor of Psychiatry at the University of Virginia Medical School, describes the great dreams from the past that have led to political innovation, scientific invention, philosophic and artistic inspiration, as well as religious illumination. Such great dreams do not have to be relics of the past. They also happen today. You can have them.

The essential method is to begin to relax in bed and use your image of your ideal to get into an inspirational frame of mind. While in that mood, let the elements of your problem dance in your mind's eye, just as John did in his hypnotic session. Then let them go, and allow yourself to have a daydream about your problem and its solution. Finally, let that daydream go, and allow yourself to drift to sleep. In the morning, write down whatever you remember of your dreaming, no matter how irrelevant or trivial it may seem. As you ponder this dream, you may be surprised to discover that it speaks more to your problem than you initially suspected.

I have researched several methods for obtaining inspirational dreams and how to work with them. I have described these approaches in *Getting Help From Your Dreams* and *The Dream Quest Workbook*. Of all the methods for seeding a dream, research has shown that using presleep suggestion and imagery is the most critical ingredient. In the previous chapter, we noted that the presleep state was an ideal condition for responding to suggestions. The use of imagery, as in the inspiration formula, is a natural extension of this fact and has been found, in countless experiments, to have a profound impact on a person's ability to have dreams about a desired topic.

If you have trouble remembering dreams, you can use the imagery method to help you recall them. As you lie in bed, imagine yourself waking up in the morning and writing down a dream. When you do wake up, immediately write down whatever is on your mind, regardless of whether or not you consider it to be a dream. If you will make a commitment to write one full page of thoughts and feelings immediately upon awakening, and follow through with this commitment for seven days in a row, I can almost guarantee that before the week is up, you will find that one morning you are writing down a dream.

The Power of Visualization

Dana and his father had just purchased an antique bicycle. It was one of those from the turn of the century, with a large front wheel almost five feet in diameter. It was a rusty bike, and many of its parts were in need of replacement. It took them six months of leisurely work to restore the bicycle to mint condition and to make it operable.

All during the period of restoration, Dana wondered if he would be able to ride that bike. It was quite tall and unwieldy. He had tried riding a bicycle like his, belonging to members of the High Wheelers Club, but he had found it almost impossible, and somewhat frightening. It wasn't going to be easy, but Dana was determined.

Dana began to dream about the bicycle. In his dreams, he struggled to climb up on the bike and ride it. He dreamed time and again of riding the bicycle, experiencing its balance, experiencing its height, experiencing the thrill.

When the day came that the bicycle was completed, Dana and his father wheeled it out of the garage and onto the

street. He remembered his dream experiences of climbing
up onto the bike and pushing off down the street. This
would be the moment of truth. He gave the bike a push as
he climbed on from the rear, and he was off and riding! On
the very first try, Dana was riding comfortably atop the
high-wheeler.

Dana told me about this experience as he was teaching
me to ride his bicycle. I can verify what a nerve-racking
experience it is to climb aboard that very tall wheel. Dana
was convinced that it was his practice sessions in his dreams
that enabled him to ride his bike from the very first day.

Dana had discovered the power of visualization from his
experience with dreams. Practicing something in the imagination pays off when the real test comes. In one study,
student basketball players attempted to improve their free-
throw shooting. One group practiced the free-throw shots
for an hour every day. Another group practiced the same
amount of time, but only in their imagination. In their
mind's eye, they would see themselves standing at the line
holding the ball. They would see the basket and feel the
body movements of making a perfect throw. At the end of a
week, when the students were retested, the students who
had practiced in their imagination had improved significantly
more than the students who had practiced with the real ball.

You can give yourself an immediate demonstration of this
effect. Turn your head slowly to the right as far as you can.
Make sure that you can turn it no farther. Relax your neck
muscles and see if you can't turn your head a bit farther, but
without forcing it or causing pain. Notice how far you can
turn it by sighting a spot on a distant wall. Return your head
to normal and close your eyes. In your imagination only,
very slowly turn your head to the right. Imagine the feeling
in your neck allowing you to continue turning your head
much farther than you did before. Then bring your head
back to normal. Do this imaginary head turn three times.

Then open your eyes and actually turn your head slowly to the right as far as you can. Sight with your eyes across the room and you will see that you have now turned your head farther than you were able to before. Through your imagination you have been able to acutally increase the flexibility in your neck!

Using imagery can extend the body's capacity and improve physical performance. Charles Garfield, Ph.D., describes in his book *Peak Performance* a personal experience that convinced him of the power of visualization. He found himself in the company of Olympic sports trainers from the Soviet Bloc countries and asked for a demonstration of their latest training techniques. Garfield had been a serious weight lifter in college years before, but he hadn't even been to a gym for several months. When he did work out, he could manage to lift 280 pounds. The trainers asked him if he thought he could lift 300 pounds. Garfield was reluctant, but gave it a try. It required all his effort, but he managed to do so. He was pleased with himself, but was utterly exhausted from the effort.

The trainers asked him how long it would take to get himself back in shape to be able to lift 365 pounds. He had once lifted that much weight and estimated that it would take about nine months of rigorous training to work back to that level of strength. They announced that he would do it within the hour! He said that was impossible. He had barely managed to lift 300 pounds and could do no more. Weight lifters know that it is necessary to increase weights in small increments, and what these trainers were suggesting represented more than a twenty percent increase in weight. They nevertheless proceeded with the demonstration.

They asked Garfield to lie down and relax. They guided him through imagining that his arms and legs were heavy and warm. They took him into a deeply relaxed state. Then they coached him in the visualization of every step of the

weight-lifting feat he was about to attempt. He saw the
additional weights added to the barbells. He saw himself lie
down beneath them. He visualized the feeling of his breathing, the feel of his weights, the feeling of exertion in his
arms as he made the press and the sound of the weights
landing back on their stand. He visualized the successful
completion of this experiment in every detail.

Garfield then got up and walked over to the bench. He
was quite apprehensive. Doing it in the imagination is one
thing, but to attempt it in reality was another. When he
started his lift, he balked. He just couldn't do it. The
trainers patiently talked him through a brief review of his
relaxation and visualization experience. They reviewed it a
second time.

During that second review, Garfield noted that suddenly
there was a switch in his frame of mind. It was no longer an
effort to perform the visualizations. An effortless and clear
image of his success translated into a sense of confidence.
He knew he could do it. He opened his eyes and lifted the
weight!

The Secret of Visualization

What is it about imagery that gives it such impressive
power? How is it possible to use visualization to imagine
something and have it come about?

Recall Cayce's description, discussed in Chapter Four, of
the soul's projective activity, how spiritual energy is patterned
by the mind to shape physical manifestation. Cayce insisted
that these attributes—spirit, mind and the physical—were
really all one and the same aspects of a singular reality.

His term "the imaginative forces" was a special one he
used when the emphasis was upon the creative aspect of the
soul. The imaginative forces refers to that process whereby

energy is creatively transformed into pattern. It also refers to that process whereby mental patterns are transformed into physical manifestation. Thus, the imagination is both a means of receiving new information, or the creativity of conceiving, and of manifesting, or giving birth. In other words, it has both receptive and active aspects.

The subconscious mind holds the key to working with the imaginative forces. The conscious mind can set the intention, but it must relinquish control to the subconscious mind to get the job done. The subconscious mind speaks the language of imagery, the pictorial patterns that shape the creative energies.

To see for yourself how you can expand upon the power of suggestion by use of imagery, try this experiment. Sit back and relax for a minute, then begin suggesting to yourself that you will salivate. "My mouth is becoming moist, my mouth is watering, it is becoming juicy." Let yourself feel your mouth becoming moist. See how much of a mouth-watering effect you can experience through suggestion alone.

Now try it a different way. Relax again and begin imagining a lemon. In your mind's eye, see its yellow skin. Imagine cutting it in half with a knife. Pick up one of the lemon halves and squeeze it to make beads of juice form on the surface. Now bring the lemon up to your mouth and suck on the juice. Notice just how sharp the tangy lemon juice can be. It makes you pucker. Notice how much your mouth is watering.

Imagining sucking on a lemon made your mouth water a lot more than simply giving yourself the suggstion to salivate. Verbal suggestion is somewhat effective, but when imagery is added, the suggestive power is irresistible. The response is involuntary and automatic. There is visualization's secret.

In the last chapter, when you were learning how to relax,

you imagined that your arm was heavy. That image automatically produced a relaxation effect. When you imagined sucking on a lemon, that image automatically produced salivation. If you want your body to respond in a particular way, you can imagine a situation in which such a response would be natural, and your subconscious mind will direct your body to match the image!

Learning how to make your hands warmer, for example, is easy if you imagine wearing gloves on a hot day. You can feel how sweaty your hands are inside those gloves. It has been demonstrated that learning how to increase the blood flow to the hands is an effective treatment for migraine headaches. It is also used as a training device for more advanced work in the use of imagery in healing. Garrett Porter, the boy described in Chapter One who healed himself of a brain tumor through visualization, began his self-healing work by learning how to make his hands warm.

Controlling Body Cells Through Imagery

That it is possible to control the activity of cells in your body through visualization may come as a surprise to you. Cayce indicated that every cell in your body has its portion of mind. That was a radical notion until the discovery that people could control the functioning of their body through the proper use of their mind. Learning to control the "alpha state," that particular brain-wave pattern associated with relaxation, was one of the early discoveries of the power of the mind over the body. More recent research has established even finer levels of control, down to single nerve cells!

In one experiment, described by Dr. Jeanne Acherberg, associate professor and Director of Research in Rehabilitation Science at the University of Texas Health Science

Center, in her book *Imagery in Healing*, medical students were shown colored slides of a particular class of white blood cells called neutrophils. The students saw how these cells removed waste from the bloodstream. They learned that these cells could change their "adherence factor," meaning whether the cells clung to the walls of the blood vessels or whether they released themselves from the walls and floated freely. These students then practiced visualizing these cells. After training in visualization, the students demonstrated the ability, as verified by blood tests, to command these cells either to increase or decrease their adherence factor. Their control was quite specific, because their visualizations did not affect the activity of any of the other classes of white blood cells.

Imagining Your Ideal Day

My own first experiment with a concept presented in the Cayce readings concerned visualizing my ideal day. I was visiting with Charles Thomas Cayce, Edgar's grandson and a psychologist like myself, at his farm in southern Virginia Beach. At the time, I was teaching psychology at Princeton University. Academic life was not appealing to me as much as I thought it would, and Charles Thomas Cayce used my expression of discontent as an opportunity to talk about his experiences visualizing an ideal life.

Edgar Cayce indicated that ideals were like the rudder of a ship. Without an ideal, one would drift randomly upon the sea of life. A clear ideal is needed to begin the process of creating a life more to your liking. Charles Thomas likes to think about ideals in a concrete and specific fashion, and he challenged me to try to visualize a sample day from my ideal life. He suggested that I imagine how I would spend my time, what I would *do*, not just what I might *have*. He said that when I was ready, I should write down all the events of that ideal day on a piece of paper and then put the paper away. He promised me that one day in the future I would discover that I was living that day. His promise was fulfilled.

Here are some of the things that I wrote on that piece of paper. I was living in a home of my own close to the beach. I got up in the morning and worked on my current book. I was at leisure in the afternoon, riding my bicycle, walking along the beach, or working in the garden. People came to visit me at my house in the late afternoon and early evening for counseling sessions. One night a week I taught a psychology class at a local college. Most evenings I engaged in social activities with my wife.

That is exactly the life that I am living today as I write this book. It feels like a dream come true. It is like walking about in my own visionary reality. It's a good feeling.

My ideal life did not come about overnight. It took a few years to manifest, and it came one step at a time. One of these steps makes another good story about the visionary power of the imagination.

In 1978, my wife and I were living in seasonal rental housing in Virginia Beach. We were tired of moving every season, so we decided we wanted to buy a house. We visualized this hypothetical, ideal house and wrote down on a piece of paper all its characteristics. We put the paper away.

Some months later, a crisis situation entered our lives and we decided that, ready or not, we had to find a house. We called a real estate agent and made an appointment. The next morning, my wife told me that she had dreamed of a house. She described it as full of light, and through a back window she could see water. We liked her dream image, because being on the waterfront was one of the items on our descriptive list of our ideal house.

When we met with the real estate agent, we explained our situation. We had almost no money for a down payment, or full-time jobs to qualify for a mortgage. We had great faith, however, that if we could find a house that would inspire us, we could work out those problems. The woman was amused, but having known us as rental customers for some years, she agreed to give it a try. She cautioned us that, realistically, we would have to come up with $500 to even make an offer and then we would need to get jobs fast to even have a chance at getting a mortgage. She suggested that we take a look at a house she knew would be coming on the market soon. It would give us a chance to face what we were up against.

She drove us to an unfamiliar neighborhood four blocks from the oceanfront and stopped at a house that wasn't very inspiring. We were disappointed but went inside. As we started to look around, my wife commented on how bright it was inside, how full of light. It reminded her of her dream, so we went into the rear of the house and saw outside the window that the property was indeed a waterfront place, sitting on the bank of an inland lake. This house was the one my wife had dreamed we would inhabit.

We told the agent that we wanted it and we would get right to work. We could use our MasterCard to come up with the earnest money. We would see if we could turn our part-time jobs into full-time. She was cautious and said that she would call us that night. When she called, it was with the news that she had spoken to the owner. She had negotiated a lower price for us and had arranged for the owner to provide a second mortgage. All we had to do was to come up with a twelve-thousand-dollar down payment and qualify to assume the existent mortgage.

Every night for a week we drove over to the house and sat outside in our car and meditated on the prospects of moving into this house. We began to call on friends and relatives, and with a few hundred dollars from some and a thousand dollars from others, we raised the down payment. My wife was able to increase her hours at her part-time job to approximate a full-time position. I was a substitute crisis-intervention counselor for the City of Virginia Beach, and within a couple of days a full-time position came open, which I took. We submitted the offer on the house the agent had arranged. By the time the mortgage company managed to evaluate our mortgage application, we looked quite acceptable.

There is an interesting side note that shows the fourth-dimensional quality of an idea. The neighbor across the street greeted me one day after we had moved in. She seemed to know me. She said that the year before I had been over to her house on an emergency call. Then I remembered. It was to deal with a runaway teenager. His name was Henry, my name. I remember because another social worker was also there on the case and her last name was Henry. We joked, because the name isn't that common, and there were three of us in one room. The name Henry means "ruler of the home." The house across the street from where the three Henrys met, the house my wife dreamed about, has been our happy home for the past ten years.

Can You Imagine It?

Claims about the power of imagery invariably bring up the question about a person's ability to imagine, to see mental images. Not everyone believes they can visualize.

When asked about what it means if a person doesn't remember dreams, Cayce answered that the person was being negligent. The same can be said about mental images. If you don't think you have mental imagery, you're just not paying attention.

The truth is that everyone does visualize. People do vary in the extent to which they accept the suggestions of their visualizations sufficiently to experience them as clear visual images.

Let me describe a situation that may demonstrate what I mean. Suppose you have an ordinary shoe box and a shipping crate ten feet tall and ten feet wide—in other words, a fairly small box and a pretty large box. Suppose you had two rubber bands, and you stretched one around the shoe box and the other around the shipping crate. Inspect each box to verify that when you stretch a rubber band around a box, the band contacts only four sides of the box, leaving two other sides untouched. Does the rubber band touch only four sides of the shoe box? Does the rubber band touch only four sides of the shipping crate? Would it be the same for a box that was one *mile* wide?

How long did it take you to make this mental confirmation? Did it take longer to inspect the shipping crate than the shoe box? What about the mile-wide box? With each box, the logic of the problem is the same. If the problem were approached simply in terms of the abstract logical principle, the size of the box would be irrelevant to the question being posed. To the extent that imagery is used, no matter how subtly, it takes longer to trace the path of a band around a shoe box than it does to trace that same path around a shipping crate. You may not be aware of your use of imagery, but if you can notice the difference in time it takes you to *think* about the different-size boxes, you may be able to infer that your thoughts are being governed by images. We all have imagery and use visualization. To have them appear to our mind's eye as pictures involves the same principle that we learned about suggestion. It is a matter of being willing to engage in an "as if" frame of mind. To visualize a box, simply pretend that you are looking at one. Ignore all your thoughts that are telling you that you are just *thinking* about a box, that you don't really see it. Pay attention only to what the pretending *feels like*. The more you pay attention to what the pretending feels like, and less to your thoughts, the more you will allow yourself to experience the picture image that is actually there. It *is* there. It can become more vivid as you close your eyes and relax.

The more willing you are to accept what you *do* experience as being a mental image, the more you become absorbed in that experience of your imagination, and the more vivid the imagery becomes.

Are you *willing* to experience the imagery? The question is important and to the point. You can choose whether you will focus on how what you experience is like an image, or whether you will focus on how it is *not* like an image, but more like a thought. To allow yourself to accept it as an image, to let yourself go into your pretending, you are taken into the images of the imagination.

We have come full circle, back to the issue that initiated us into this section on altered states of consciousness and the hidden powers of the mind. It is the matter of the inner will, the deeper source of will than willpower. With our conscious mind, we can direct our imagination only to a limited extent. Whether or not the images we conjure will come to life and grab our awareness depends upon a deeper will. It is more a question of our true willingness.

Confirm Your Visualizations in Action

It is hard to consistently visualize something, even something very desirable, if we are not willing to accept it as true and act accordingly. Cayce indicated that we shouldn't expect to rest upon the power of visualization alone, but need to express our intentions in action. If the key to visualization is a mental process of *acting as if* you are seeing something, then the key to manifesting visualizations is to *act as if* they will manifest.

We can demonstrate this willingness, and reinforce its suggestive power within the subconscious mind, by our conscious actions. By working with our attitudes, and taking appropriate steps in behavior, we indicate the sincerity of our desire to manifest what we imagine. My wife and I visualized our ideal house for some time, but it did not manifest until we took a step in faith and acted as if it was there and we were prepared to buy it. We made a commitment in action, and the means to follow through materialized.

Cayce would remind us of the saying "Pray hard, as if everything depended upon God, and work hard, as if everything depended upon you." It applies as well to using the hidden powers of the mind in conjunction with conscious efforts in the world. Both are required. Even to be in the right place at the right time, which some would call luck, requires getting up from the meditation chair. It is with the love of our ideal in our heart, with a vision in our mind, and with very busy hands, that we become inspired creators.

13

The Spiritual Mystery
of the Mind

*The earth then is a three-dimensional, a three-phase
or three manner expression. Just as the Father,
the Son, the Holy Spirit are one. So are our body,
mind and soul one—in Him.*

Edgar Cayce 1567-2

Is there any greater mystery than life itself? It is a wondrous,
self-perpetuating carnival. There is the magical symphony
of vibrating atoms, the gallery of masterful and stunning
landscapes, the exciting circus of animals and the infinitely
complex and varied stories of the human creatures.

The forces of nature may be blind. Life may play out its
patterns in an unknowing and automatic reflex chain of
electromagnetic and atomic actions and reactions. Yet the
human being is aware. We behold the bounty of life. We are
conscious of our existence. The players in the cause and
effect sequence of the life of chemistry and physics may not
question why they act the way they do, but we humans
notice, we question, and we are filled with wonder.

If there is a mystery to life, it is because there is human consciousness to pose the question. What is the purpose of life? What is the story? What is going on? And who are we? What does it mean that we are aware of ourselves, that we know we are conscious?

A Key To the Universe

What if out of the swirl of creation there appeared a clue to the puzzle of life? What if in the midst of all the elements and their varied formations there appeared in nature a magical sculpture that revealed the secret of the universe? Its features and the patterns in its construction expressed the Creator's signature. Its movements revealed the Creator's thoughts and feelings. When properly addressed, it shone forth with pictures upon a magical screen that was a veritable encyclopedia of the secrets of the universe. What a prize this sculpture would be!

There is such a sculpture. It's the human being—it's you and me. Cayce revealed that the human being is a mirror of creation. Within our very being, sometimes right before our eyes and sometimes buried deeply within the unconscious, lie all the secrets of the universe.

It may surprise you, but of all these secrets there is none greater than that God exists! It is the cornerstone to understanding creation and our role in it. We are like time capsules created by God, ready at any moment to break out of our shell of material egocentricity and give expression to God's intention in creating us.

Cayce tells us that it is God's intention that we be companions with the Creator. In full realization of our true essence, with full awareness of our oneness with God, the purpose of our coming into being is to share in the responsibility of continuing the process of creation, to add to the glory of life by the way we channel God's creative energy that flows through us.

Each human being is one of God's experiments in conscious living, each having a portion of the divine energy, or spirit, a mind and a free will by which to make choices and accept influences. Each of us represents God's attempt to become aware, in a finite material body, of the nature of the infinite creative forces. Each of our experiences is therefore very important to God, and within our being we can sense the Creator's reaction to our responses to those experiences.

God awaits our recognition. The meeting comes within. The honoring of God is to be expressed outwardly, in our thoughts and actions toward the rest of creation.

The Prime Directive

Deep down we are more alike than different. We share with the animals various survival instincts. Among one another, we share the need for love and companionship; we all face the task of leaving our parents and making our own way in the world. We all face death. Most of our personal experiences, though they seem personal to us, have a universal, archetypal heritage. If you have ever shared deeply with another person your experiences in life, especially your feelings about these experiences, you most likely have discovered that your confidant had similar feelings. The human story is universal, even though no two are identical.

One of the common dimensions of human experience is the attempt to reconcile the need for security with the desire for freedom. We all long for the freedom to be ourselves, to express our individual creativity. On the other hand, we realize that we need to make a place for ourselves in the world if we are to survive. The need for security compels us to fit in with society, to do what is expected. Complying with the needs of the whole sometimes requires our sacrificing what would be good for us as individuals.

This universal human experience has an important spiritual dimension. God expresses in multiple individualities. God is millions upon millions of souls, and then some. Each soul is an expression of God, an individual and unique expression. The life of an individual human being is a symbolic manifestation of its soul. Each human being has the potential to reveal its spiritual origin in a unique way. That, in fact, is the task God sets before each of us.

As Cayce explains it, we are all One in God, yet each of us, as souls, is a unique creation. Our task in life is to develop and express this individuality while at the same time expressing that Oneness of God, who is our essential identity. The primary commandment is to love God and to love our neighbors as ourselves. Each of us is to do this in our own individual way. Yet there is only one way to comply with this commandment. It is to be yourself.

It is a paradoxical and contradictory assignment, at least to the conscious mind. On the one hand, it is such an easy and natural task that a baby does it quite instinctively. We grown-ups, on the other hand, find it an almost impossible job. Perhaps that is why we have to become again as children in order to know how to do it.

To be yourself, with no holding back, requires self-acceptance and a lack of anxious self-consciousness. Giving no thought to your separate self, life itself becomes your self, and you accept being one with that experience. In that way, you bridge the opposites of the paradox, living life like no one but you can, while embracing in a spirit of love all of life. That life is God. It is you.

Experiencing and loving life as yourself, you naturally reach out with whatever unique perceptions and talents you have and serve that life. You do this in your own unique way, expressing your individuality. Your link to life is your security; your expression of your uniqueness is your freedom. You can have it all. All you have to do is become aware that the You we're talking about is not the little separate you constructed by your conscious mind. It is the bigger You, the divine You.

Your soul grew that separate, little you in order to better experience itself in fuller awareness. Let that separate you be a tool of your soul, not a runaway caricature of your true essence, a tragic illusion, the Sorcerer's Apprentice up to its ears in its own mess. The conscious mind is an able servant and apprentice of the soul. The Prime Directive is to act accordingly. To follow it willingly is to awaken to awareness of the blessings of co-creatorship.

The Holographic Soul of Reality

Cayce's primary teaching on the soul is that it is both a piece of God as well as a miniature replica of its Creator, and thus a model of the whole of creation. But how can something be broken into pieces so that it also still reflects the whole thing? How can it be that we are each separate and unique, yet all essentially one and the same being? Edgar Cayce's teachings on the soul and the projection of reality through consciousness has recently gained a new source of support. We can now think about his teachings on this subject with a new conceptual tool, thanks to modern technology.

Cayce predicted that the crystal would someday be the source of an important invention. The use of a ruby crystal to create a laser beam has indeed led to many important inventions. In particular, laser holography, the exciting three-dimensional image-projection system, has provided an even more magical image of the creative power of consciousness. This advance in technology has also led to new theories on the nature of consciousness itself and its role in creating what we perceive as reality. Holographic theory parallels Cayce's teachings in many important respects.

The hologram has proven to be an even more astounding example of how the part can reflect the whole. Here is how it works.

When a normal camera takes a picture, it uses a lens to focus the light reflected off an object before it is allowed to expose the light-sensitive film. The result is a two-dimensional picture, reflecting only what can be seen of the object from the camera's momentary perspective.

In laser-beam holography, no camera lens is used. The laser beam itself is already highly focused. To take a picture of an object, the laser beam is shot at the object and a photographic plate picks up the light as it bounces off the object. To show the picture, a laser beam is aimed at the developed photographic plate. The markings on the plate cause the laser light to bounce off it in a way that casts an image of the original object out in space. No screen is used. The object appears as a lifelike, three-dimensional form. You can walk around the image and see it from all sides. It literally appears to exist as a real object, an illusion of the real thing!

In a normal, two-dimensional picture, there is an exact correspondence between a spot on the picture and the portion of the object shown. The top of the object appears on the top of the picture. If you cut the top off the picture, you lose the top of the object. In a holographic picture, there is no such correspondence. The laser light reflected from the original object is allowed to scatter all over the photographic plate. As a result, and here is the surprise, every piece of the plate contains the whole picture.

You can cut up the plate in hundreds of pieces. Each

piece contains a unique set of patterns as a function of its position on the plate when the exposure was made. No two pieces are alike. On the other hand, if you shine the laser light on just one of those pieces, you will still get a three-dimensional projection of the *whole object* out in space. All that is affected by using smaller and smaller pieces of the original whole plate is that the sharpness of the image begins to get a bit fuzzy, but it still remains the whole image. Here is a modern, technological equivalent of Cayce's concept of a soul as being both a piece of the Creator and an image of the whole!

Many theorists have pointed to the holographic phenomenon as a suggestive image to explain the universal mystical experience of oneness. The hologram has become a metaphor for the transpersonal mind and has shed new light on ESP. It suggests a new way to understand the nature of consciousness.

According to Cayce's model, consciousness is a projection of the soul and the reality we experience is like a dream upon an invisible movie screen. The discovery of the hologram has led to the development of a scientific theory of consciousness much like Cayce's perspective. Karl Pribram, a brain scientist at Stanford University, has concluded that the brain must operate like a hologram. For one thing, we are learning that memories are not stored in any one particular place in the brain. You can cut out large chunks of the brain and still find the memories intact. The memories are stored all over the brain, just as a holograhic image is repeated countless times all over the holographic plate.

Cayce indicated that the brain resonates to vibrations. Dr. Pribram has come to the same conclusion. He theorizes that the brain interprets vibrations both from the world of stimuli through the senses as well as from the world of ideas that exist in another dimension. Consciousness operates through the brain like the laser light striking the holographic plate. The result in both cases is similar: a three-dimensional image projeced out into the appearance of space. Pribram is saying that we do literally experience holographic movies, living dreams created by our brains.

Spiritual Use of the Creation Formula

The stunning, illusory reality of the holographic image gives added meaning to Cayce's formula of creation. The spirit of the laser beam, cast through the holographic mind, projects the reality of manifestation in the three-dimensional realm.

We have learned how to apply this formula in both the conscious and subconscious mind. Through the setting of an ideal and the cultivation of a corresponding attitude, we can shape our behaviors to construct a life of our choosing. Through suggestion and visualization, we can tap into the hidden powers of the mind to create manifestations of our choosing. We can create an ideal life for ourselves.

The Prime Directive would ask us to be mindful of our spiritual mission. It can be achieved through the choosing of an ideal that includes a vision of the interrelatedness of life, that reflects the spirit of love. No matter how much power we can attain through the use of the mind, no matter how much understanding or psychic ability, how would it benefit us if we didn't learn the secret of love? Only in learning to love will we gain entry to the paradise that life offers. Otherwise, we will find ourselves imprisoned in a world of our own making, a lonely world of self-absorption and self-defense. It is to our benefit, as well as a benefit to life, for us to use the creative formula of the mind in a manner based upon an ideal of love.

If we are willing to submit voluntarily to the Prime Directive, if we are willing to do what is necessary to act in acceptant patience, love, and cooperation with the whole of life, with all circumstances that we meet, we will find that such an ideal will carry us through any of the circumstances that we might confront. It will save us the aggravation of doubt and fear. It will leave us free to enjoy life.

The Christ Consciousness

Cayce indicates that if we were to adopt such an ideal to guide the use of our creative energies, we would receive more than enough help from that ideal to transform our lives. When we work with an ideal, the ideal works with us.

Cayce gave many psychic readings on the life of Jesus and its meaning for the development of humanity's consciousness. In distinction to the historical person, Cayce also refers to the Christ Consciousness, an exalted state of mind that Jesus developed within himself.

God incarnates in each and every one of us. What was special about Jesus was that he was directly aware of his oneness with the Creator. This awareness was not just an assumption or a concept, but as a living reality. In developing the Christ Consciousness, Jesus fulfilled God's intention that a human being could simultaneously manifest in a material, three-dimensional ego consciousness while simultaneously living in oneness with God. Jesus willingly carried the cross of the Prime Directive and discovered the integration of the two levels of experience, the earthly and the heavenly.

Jesus died on that cross, but he also had a rebirth experience. In his teachings, Jesus made many references to the theme of death and rebirth. The seed must surrender its self-contained shell and crack open if the plant is to sprout.

As the ego yields its fearful defensiveness of its self-contained reality to the love of life itself, a wider consciousness is expressed. The kingdom of Heaven lies within, waiting patiently for us to die to it. Cayce indicates that we practice that process every night, as we fall asleep and awaken into the soul's consciousness, the dream.

Less common, but receiving more attention in recent years, are the experiences of near-death. Perhaps as a result of an accident, a heart attack, or during surgery, a person dies, but is revived within a few minutes. Many people who have been brought back from death have reported incredible visions of beings of light and environments of infinite love, peace, and tranquility. As astounding as such experiences may be, what is more important is the impact that such experiences have had on these reborn individuals. They report they have lost any fear of death. They now *know* that consciousness survives; they have *experienced* their oneness with life. Their personal values change. They become less concerned with material things, less interested in competition or in winning recognition and approval. They feel at peace with themselves and are more interested in the quality of their daily experience. They spend more time enjoying loving interactions with others; they find they are more naturally concerned with the welfare of others. Many also discover their psychic ability, especially that of healing.

The movie *It's a Wonderful Life* provides a touching, and instructive, portrayal of the effects of a near-death experience. The character played by Jimmy Stewart was about to commit suicide because of financial difficulties when an angel gave him an unusual review of his life. He was able to see what life would have been like for all his friends and loved ones had he never been born. Although the man thought his life had been a failure, he saw that, in fact, his very presence had been an important influence on the lives of others in ways he had never considered. He had to

surrender his narrow focus on financial matters and accept a
larger perspective on the meaning of a life.

The development of the Christ Consciousness doesn't
necessarily involve a dramatic flash of light. The surrender
of the little self doesn't always mean a total renunciation of
our personal concerns. It can mean getting out of our own
way, getting past self-*preoccupation* and making allowances
for the fact that we have more to offer to life than just our
accomplishments.

The Mind Is the Way

Near-death experiences confirm the fact that the Christ
Consciousness is a potential hidden within the mind of all of
us, regardless of our particular religious faith. To develop
the Christ Consciousness, we do not have to have a near-
death experience. Nor do we have to suffer the trials of
crucifixion. If we can accept pain and suffering as the
inescapable chafing of the truth against the shell of our
defended egos, we can ask of any experience that it teach us
something, that it help release us into the fuller light of the
truth of our ideal. It is a matter of attitude. Our frame of
mind is the key to the Christ Consciousness.

In his readings on the mysteries of the mind, Cayce often
made reference to a certain analogy between God and the
human being. He explained that in our three-dimensional
world, we experience God as Father, Son, and Holy Spirit.
Likewise, he explained, we humans are as a body, a mind,
and a soul. The Father dimension of God is like our body,
our soul is like the Holy Spirit, and our mind is like the
Son. In other words, Cayce identified the mind as being like
the Son of God.

Such an analogy makes the mind extremely important and
reveals its spiritual significance. Jesus insisted that no one

could get to God except through Him. Cayce explained
this statement in a way that is similar to other modern
theologians and psychologists of religious experience. Even
though every human being is a part of God, a child of
God, we experience God directly only through the intermediary of our higher self as it develops the Christ Consciousness. This development requires, Cayce indicated,
that every atom in the body resonate harmoniously with
the ideal.

The conscious mind plays a vital role in this development.
It is the conscious mind that decides to work with an ideal.
It is the conscious mind that focuses the effort to develop
constructive attitudes and habits. It is the conscious mind
that can invite into awareness the deeper levels of consciousness.

The conscious mind can direct the development of the
will to come into accord with the ideal. In the Bible,
Paul laments that although he chooses to do right, he
often does otherwise. He concludes that he must "die
daily" in order that Christ may live within him. In other
words, he chooses to surrender to his higher power to
develop his will. He imagines and believes that this higher
power will come to direct his actions, and he is willing to
have it so.

Cayce indicates that our part is to make the conscious
decision concerning what ideal we will serve. The ideal will
then help us in our efforts. The life of Jesus, Cayce
indicates, established the Christ Consciousness as a pattern
in the universal mind. That Jesus "died for our sins" means
that he found a way for a material body consciousness to
submit to God's will. The way he found is now available as
a pattern in the fourth-dimensional domain of ideas and
ideals. It is a pattern within the superconcious mind capable
of influencing and guiding our own consciousness, should
we choose to invite it.

Becoming Channels of the Higher Self

One recent afternoon I accompanied my friend Jim to
pick up his five-year-old daughter, Jessica, at school. Loaded with papers, she climbed into the back seat of the car. As
we drove away, Jessica reached forward between the two
front seats, announcing, "Here, Daddy, this is for you!"
She presented him with a cutout drawing of a person in the
form of a flower that she had made. The colorful flower
person was smiling happily. So was the artist, as well as the
artist's father, who commented, "She's the master of all she
surveys, and she shares it willingly."

I marveled at the innocent beauty and joy of Jessica's
creation. She created out of the joy of her own experience,
and her sharing her work brought joy to us all. Her handing
her unique creation to her father as a gift of love seemed such
an exquisite image conveying the spirit of Cayce's revelation
about the human being. We are like flowers, drawing upon the
life energy of the sun and patterning it, each in our own way,
to create love offerings of beauty to those we meet.

The incredible powers of the mind are for us to use as we
choose. Each of us perceives the world with a uniquely
creative subjectivity. How we see things, and react to them,
not only determines our own experience, but is also our gift
to the events of the world. With our imagination, we can
reach out to an infinite realm of possibilities and cast a wish
upon whatever star suits our fancy. If we are willing to
make the effort, we can channel the creative potential of that
vision into a living reality.

When we focus on the highest values and stretch ourselves to share our best efforts with others, we complete a
circuit that allows the life energy to adventure forth into
new patterns of being. Our own awareness is expanded as

we become channels of our higher self, servants of our souls' quest toward the long-lost paradise on earth. If such would be your ideal, if you can imagine it, if you are willing, then act as if it were so, knowing that the thoughts of your heart will come to pass. That is the way of the mysteries of the mind.

Suggested Reading

Cayce, Hugh Lynn. *Venture Inward*. New York: Harper & Row, 1964.

Cayce, Hugh Lynn. *Faces of Fear*. San Francisco: Harper & Row, 1980.

Hudson, Thomson Jay. *The Law of Psychic Phenomena*. New York: Samuel Weiser, 1969.

Jampolsky, Gerald G. *Love Is Letting Go of Fear*. Millbrae, CA: Celestial Arts, 1979.

Pike, Cynthia. *The Miracle of Suggestion: The Story of Jennifer*. Virginia Beach: Inner Vision Publishing, 1988.

Puryear, Herbert. *The Edgar Cayce Primer: Discovering the Path to Self-Transformation*. New York: Bantam Books, 1982.

Puryear, Herbert, and Thurston, Mark. *Meditation and the Mind of Man*. Virginia Beach: A.R.E. Press, 1978.

Reed, Henry. *Getting Help From Your Dreams*. New York: Ballantine Books, 1988.

Reed, Henry. *Awakening Your Psychic Powers: Edgar Cayce's*

Wisdom for the New Age. San Francisco: Harper & Row, 1988.

Reed, Henry. *Channeling Your Higher Self*. New York: Warner Books, 1989.

Rossi, Ernest Lawrence. *The Psychobiology of Mind-Body Healing: New Concepts of Therapeutic Hypnosis*. New York: Norton, 1986.

Siegel, Bernie. *Love, Medicine and Miracles*. New York: Harper & Row, 1986.

Thurston, Mark. *Paradox of Power: Balancing Personal and Higher Will*. Virginia Beach: A.R.E. Press, 1987.

THE A.R.E. TODAY
■ ■ ■

The Association for Research and Enlightenment, Inc., is a non-profit, open membership organization committed to spiritual growth, holistic healing, psychical research and its spiritual dimensions; and more specifically, to making practical use of the psychic readings of the late Edgar Cayce. Through nationwide programs, publications and study groups, A.R.E. offers all those interested, practical information and approaches for individual study and application to better understand and relate to themselves, to other people and to the universe. A.R.E. membership and outreach is concentrated in the United States with growing involvement throughout the world.

The A.R.E. facilities, located at 67th Street and Atlantic Avenue, are open year-round. Visitors are always welcome and may write A.R.E., P.O. Box 595, Virginia Beach, VA 23451, for more information about the Association.

For all UK general enquiries, newsletter and study group information contact: Edgar Cayce Centre, PO Box 8, Stanley, County Durham, DH9 7XQ.